Promoting Your Music

The Lovin' of the Game

Tom May and Dick Weissman

Routledge
Taylor & Francis Group
New York   London

Routledge
Taylor & Francis Group
270 Madison Avenue
New York, NY 10016

Routledge
Taylor & Francis Group
2 Park Square
Milton Park, Abingdon
Oxon OX14 4RN

© 2007 by Taylor & Francis Group, LLC
Routledge is an imprint of Taylor & Francis Group, an Informa business

Printed in the United States of America on acid-free paper
10 9 8 7 6 5 4 3 2 1

International Standard Book Number-13: 978-0-415-97757-9 (Softcover) 978-0-415-97756-2 (Hardcover)

Library of Congress Cataloging-in-Publication Data

May, Tom.
   Promoting your music : the lovin' of the game / Tom May, Dick Weissman.
     p. cm.
     Includes bibliographical references (p.   ).
     ISBN 978-0-415-97756-2 -- ISBN 978-0-415-97757-9
    1. Popular music--Vocational guidance. 2. Music trade--Vocational guidance. I. Weissman, Dick. II. Title.

ML3795.M32 2007
780.23'73--dc22
                                       2007000041

**Visit the Taylor & Francis Web site at
http://www.taylorandfrancis.com**

**and the Routledge Web site at
http://www.routledge.com**

I saw the feather river glide over shining golden sand,
Struck a silver ribbon wide, held a million in my hand.
But beside the lookin' for, well the findin' is always tame
And there's nothing drives a gambler
  like the lovin' of the game.
All my life I ran around searching hard from town to town
But I never ever found anything to tie me down.
Still I wouldn't trade my time for a solid diamond claim
No, I would not trade a fortune for the lovin' of the game.
So long, darling, don't you cry, I hope
  that things pan out for you,
All the good times going by, got to have ourselves a few.
Where I'm going has no end, what I'm seeking has no name.
No, the treasure's not the takin', it's the lovin' of the game.
No, the treasure's not the takin', it's the lovin' of the game.

CONTENTS

FOREWORD

Nadia Boulanger wrote, "Nothing is better than music. . . . It has done more for us than we have the right to hope for." If you are holding this book and reading these words, you probably agree with Nadia. You probably also agree with Beethoven who said, "Life without music would be a mistake." You know that music has led you to friends and adventure. You know that it has provided comfort and emotional catharsis. You know that you can't live, or don't want to live, without it. But you are wondering whether you can make a living with it, even part time. You are wondering if there are actions to take and decisions to make in order to connect your songs to the audiences for which they are suited. Although you enjoy performing "covers" of other writers' songs, you would rather share your own songs and are wondering if there are places where they might be savored and appreciated rather than ignored in the haze and the noise of a tedious bar gig. You're seeking listeners in a world where they seem to have moved on and gone home.

When I was a kid, I wanted to be Hank Williams. I was only nine, but after I saw the 1965 movie *Your Cheating Heart,* I dreamed of strumming a guitar and yodeling in a white suit decorated with musical notes. It looked like fun and maybe it would make that blonde-haired girl in class like me. I think I was the only nine-year-old in my Philadelphia suburb with this dream, but it helped sustain me through the tortures of math and Little League.

A decade later, I wanted to be Woody Guthrie. His 1943 autobiography, *Bound for Glory,* and the 1976 movie of the same name, knocked me down and stirred me up, and I knew that hitting the road with a guitar would be a romantic adventure, with more freedom and better scenery than a "real" job. I yearned to hop freights in western states, to sing about outlaws, unions, cowboys, and hard travelin', while maybe changing the world along the way.

But there was already a Hank, already a Woody, so I just learned their songs, wrote some of my own, and grew up to be me instead. That includes being a folksinger/songwriter, and occasional guitar player—certainly thanks to Hank and Woody, as well as to John Denver, Jim Croce, Gordon Lightfoot, Mary McCaslin, David Mallett, Bill Staines, and my parents, Helen and Ed, who bought me a Sears guitar on which I learned a handful of chords that have served me well through the years.

Writing songs, singing other people's songs, either solo or with a friend or two on a coffeehouse stage, by a summer night's campfire, or in a sing-along living room, became a regular part of my life. Choosing the singer/songwriter path led to absurd frustrations such as catching the wrong train to get to a gig that didn't exist in a town not on the map, and making too many phone calls to people who didn't want to hear from me for break-even gigs, in places with thick smoke and loud espresso machines. But following that singer/songwriter path also led to love and adventure, to meeting most of the folks who matter the most to me, and to some of the prettiest ZIP codes in the country.

I only play about two dozen gigs a year. If a gig looks like it might be fun, profitable, help a good cause, or some combination of those three, I'll pull out my Gibson J-200, recall some lyrics, show up early, set up the PA, and hope for the best. Sometimes I'll look in the rearview mirror of my car and see my guitar and duffel bag in the backseat and smile to think that, despite my "real job" in academia, I haven't completely forsaken the Hank and Woody troubadour dreams of my youth.

But you have troubadour dreams of your own and the book you're holding—written by two folk music veterans—can help you make them come true. Tom May has been a singer/songwriter/guitarist for more than three decades, experiencing many different aspects of the vocation: performing in countless venues from bars to concert halls, organizing festivals, hosting the *River City Folk* radio and television programs, releasing his CDs, producing CDs for other artists, arranging tours, opening shows for the likes of Gordon Lightfoot and Willie Nelson, and figuring out what to do when his car's transmission disintegrates 16 miles east of Cheyenne, Wyoming, with gigs looming in Nebraska. Dick Weissman recently left his gig as an associate professor of music business management at the University of Colorado in Denver. He is an accomplished banjo player who has written several books about music, released albums on the Folk Era label, and served as producer and musician on the recordings of other artists. More than four decades ago, Weissman joined with John Phillips and Scott MacKenzie to form the Journeymen, a popular folk music group of the early 1960s. They recorded a couple of albums and toured the folk music circuit. (Phillips went on to form the Mamas and the Papas and MacKenzie later topped the charts with his "San Francisco" song, in which we're advised to wear some flowers in our hair if we're going there.) Both Tom May and Dick Weissman have experienced many trials and triumphs in the field during their long careers; here's your chance to learn from them before going out and having some of your own.

There are no guarantees in life but there are likelihoods. It's just more likely that we will be more successful and fulfilled in our own endeavors after closely considering the wisdom of people who have been doing similar endeavors full time for a long time. Considering May and Weissman's insights can save us some time, money, and frustration. Their insights can help us devise our own plans and find our own paths as we try to find a place for our songs. If Nadia was right about there being nothing better than music, and if Beethoven was right about the mistake of living life without it, then we should figure out as many ways as we can to nurture it, share it, and keep the songs out there on the wind somewhere.

Although there is no single road that leads from your guitar and notepad in the kitchen to the gigs where people are requesting your songs rather than someone else's, this book can help you find your own way to that destination. We singer/songwriters are often naïve, or simply distracted thinking of new tunes, forgetting that we need to make phone calls and promote ourselves if we want gigs on the calendar several months later. We need to think about microphones and wiring our guitars for sound, or recording a CD and sending it to periodicals where maybe a kind writer will say nice things about it. We need to pull out maps and check if it's possible to drive from Moose, Wyoming to Los Angeles in two days, while hoping there's a noncasino, folk music gig available in Las Vegas on the way. We need to know how to get paid royalties just in case somebody records our songs or if they're played on the radio. We need to know about signing contracts where agreements are written down in black and white regarding money, sound systems, lodging, and what happens if a blizzard closes the road.

In this book, May and Weissman help you with these decisions and details—and other things we forget to remember—in their honest, conversational, and friendly style. Their tips, tricks, warnings, and insights can save you some time, money, and frustration. I wish there had been a book like this when I was wandering around the country, walking into cafes and bars with my guitar, asking to see the manager; it would have saved me from some dead ends and locked doors. I hope it does that for you.

And when you're done with the book, get back to work! There are places to go, songs to be written, audiences waiting for you somewhere down the road. I wish you all the best, but the unexpected can occur around the next bend—so if your transmission disintegrates near Rock Springs, Wyoming, give me a call.

Chris Kennedy
Rock Springs, Wyoming

1

JUST STARTING OUT
Background and Important Information

So you have decided you might want to be a performing singer/songwriter?

You may have been impressed by someone you heard on *American Idol* who said she wrote the song that she performed, or perhaps you have sung in church for years and been encouraged to go out and present your music to a wider audience, or maybe those gigs at the local tavern have been so much fun you want to turn it into a living and a lifestyle.

Whatever the case may be, it is a challenging yet potentially very rewarding life. It is fiercely competitive; if you are looking for great financial rewards, the chances of that are unpredictable. The great rewards of a career as a performing singer/songwriter lie in the experiences you will have and the friends you will make pursuing that goal in your life, as well as in the joy of creativity and seeing yourself grow as an artist.

However, there are ways you can increase your chances of being able to make a living as a songwriter/performer, if that is what you decide to do. There are also lessons to be learned from the artists and other persons interviewed in this book that should give you the confidence you need to move on to the next level, whatever that means for you.

Rather than trying to be a compendium of music theory, specific rhyming patterns, or formulas for writing the next hit song, this book is meant to be a portrait of the lifestyle of being a performing singer/songwriter, including commentary by artists who have and are still doing it in a successful manner, and some ideas on how you can get to that point. This is not a book that portrays the brief trajectory of pop music stars, but rather how some artists have succeeded in carving out a fulfilling career in an art form they believe in.

Some of these people have been successful in making their careers financially secure, and others have chosen to carve a less lucrative but just as rewarding path.

Becoming a songwriter, performer, or both is never a rational business decision. That is not to say it cannot be a profitable lifestyle, but the outcome is difficult to predict, no matter how talented you are.

There are many different ways to pursue this multifaceted, complicated business. In this chapter, I portray three different styles of being a singer/songwriter—but bear in mind there are many other ways to mix and match lifestyles and turn your avocation or passion for songs into either a career or an enjoyable sideline activity in your life.

Steve Gillette has some excellent words of advice in his book *Songwriting and the Creative Process,* advice that echoes my own feelings on this task that has the ability to touch so many lives:

> There are many good reasons and creative activity that cannot be justified in terms of the top forty charts. If as songwriters we can connect with the immense energy and emotional truth in the heart of each of us waiting to be expressed and acknowledged, there is no limit to what a song can accomplish.

At the bottom of every bit of experience, advice, and instruction in this book, I hope that is what we are all striving for as songwriters.

DIFFERENT KINDS OF COMPOSERS
Full-Time New York/Nashville/Los Angeles Nonperforming Songwriters

This category is probably the smallest numerically. Some of the recognizable names in this division would be Harlan Howard, the well-known country songwriter, with dozens of #1 country hits; the late Cindy Walker, who wrote many of the songs that became hits for groups such as the Sons of the Pioneers and Gene Autry; and Diane Warren, who is probably the most successful nonperforming singer/songwriter today, with songs recorded by the Jefferson Airplane, Bon Jovi, and many other top groups.

This is the category that many music fans, housewives, and amateur singer/songwriters are convinced will bring them great riches. It is not a precise science by any means, and placing songs has more to do with music business connections and timing and less to do with the merit of the composition.

Placing a song with a music publisher in hopes of eventually having it land on a major artist's album is indeed a long shot. There are many books that describe in depth how to go about this and give you the requirements that publishers request when you submit material, who is accepting songs, what kind of songs are being reviewed, and so forth. Some of these books are listed in the Bibliography and Musician Resources section at the end of this book, and are well worth researching for specific information.

If you are an unpublished songwriter, the best single tool to help you is the annual guide *Songwriter's Market*. It contains a large list of publishers, including some of their credits, addresses, phone numbers, e-mails, and so on. Every publisher in the book has agreed to accept unsolicited material or specifically state they will not accept such material. Any complaint against a publisher is investigated by the editors of the book; if they receive more than two complaints, they drop the publisher from next year's book. We talk more extensively about this publication in later chapters, and complete information on it is available in the bibliography.

Here are a couple of useful hints that will help you to use the book; they mostly involve using common sense. If you see a rap music publisher in northern Idaho, you should be particularly careful in reviewing his credits. How much of a rap business exists there? Another no–no is to spot a publisher whose credits are all with the same record company, one that you have never heard of. Chances are that this publisher *owns* the record company, and these are not commercial records but glorified publishers' demos.

It is a good idea to check to see that anyone mentioned in the listing still works at the company. You can search for the company on the Internet, send an e-mail, or make a phone call. Nothing marks you as an amateur faster than writing to someone who left a company months or years ago.

Use every resource and tool you can access, because there are hundreds of nonperforming songwriters in Nashville, Los Angeles, and New York, working subsistence jobs and ceaselessly barraging publishers and producers with material. These writers are very committed to succeeding and are cultivating music business connections and making contacts on a daily basis. Even so, only a tiny percentage of them will place songs with a major-label artist.

For the lucky few who do, the songwriting mechanical royalty (album sales), as of 2006, is 9.1 cents per unit, or 1.75 cents per minute, whichever amount is greater.

Airplay royalties are dependent upon rules that are constantly being renegotiated by the professional rights organizations (the American Society of Composers, Authors, and Publishers [ASCAP], Broadcast Music Incorporated [BMI], the Society of European Songwriters, Artists, and Composers [SESAC], the Composers, Authors, and Publishers Association of Canada [CAPAC], and others). As a general rule, a crossover hit (a song that is on the top of the charts in more than one category of music) can net the songwriter/publisher $250,000 or more. Many of these kinds of songs become even more valuable over a long period of time as they are used for other purposes such as ad campaigns, movie scores, and other media.

These outlets can bring in an income of more than a million dollars for a single song. Future uses and airplay of a song can bring in considerable money for many years.

Songs are administered and placed by publishing companies, which generally take half of the proceeds for their trouble. Publishing contracts with writers are as varied in their terms as the number of songs that are written, but that 50 percent figure is a general rule of thumb, split between the publisher and composer.

Publishing companies and producers are the key to placing songs with major-label artists. Most of the recording artists who are not songwriters themselves rely very heavily on the judgment of their producers to choose songs. Again, more often than not, those songs recommended by their producers will be placed due to some personal connection with the writer that has been made.

Some publishers even have staff songwriters. These writers are given a monthly stipend, and for that sum they are expected to turn out a dozen or so acceptable songs per year for the publishing company that has them on staff. The stipend is deducted from any eventual royalty that the songs generate.

So you can see that if you are competing in the world of the non-performing songwriter, the competition will be substantial. This is not to say it cannot be done, but it is best to approach the challenge with a sense of realism and knowledge of the odds.

Most performing singer/songwriters, including myself, have hoped that at various times in our lives, particularly when raising a family, we could take a little time off of the road and let our songs do the work for us. "Mailbox money" is the term I first heard for those kinds of pleasant postal surprises.

Eliza Gilkyson says of that time in her life,

If I had achieved any success in pitching my songs, I might have just worked as a songwriter. I would have loved to have done that when I was raising my kids. I never had the contacts. I still don't know how to get the songs to people. I still don't have music business friends; I have lots of musician friends. I'm not really part of the music business scene; I never have been. The way songs get placed with other artists, from what I've seen over the years, comes from knowing and creating connections. I never wanted to live in Nashville. I am not good at targeting people as marks for me to work, to try to get my needs met.

I believe that is true for most songwriters; we are not necessarily the best people to pitch our own work, and we generally do not have the connections it takes to get a song placed.

Finding an established publisher who believes in your songs and is willing to take them on is the best way to place them with recording artists. You need a demo recording of your songs so that the publisher can evaluate your work.

If you are not an accomplished performer yourself, you are going to have to pay to have a demo that represents your songs in the best light possible. Expect to spend $1000 up to many thousands of dollars to have a good 4-song demo produced of your original material. You can, of course, have it done by friends for less—but bear in mind that you truly get what you pay for in recording. I will talk more about the recording process in a later chapter, but if you are serious about performing and getting your songs heard by other artists and publishers, you need to do a respectable recording of them as soon as you are able to do so.

Part-Time Composers with Day Jobs, Dreams, and a Few Gigs

If the first category in the chapter would be the smallest numerically, part-time composers and performers would definitely be the largest, and a group that nearly every singer/songwriter/performer has belonged to at some point in his or her life.

Let me stress that this book highlights a few techniques that songwriters such as Gordon Lightfoot, Eliza Gilkyson, Harry Manx, I, and others have used to make our way in the music business. However, there is not a right or wrong way, but rather a thousand different styles of doing this decidedly quirky vocation.

Most all of us have had to do other professions while moving in the direction of being able to pursue music full time. If we are lucky, we

Figure 1.1 Gordon Lightfoot. Courtesy of Gordon Lightfoot and Early Morning Productions.

learn something about ourselves and become familiar with time-management tools that will serve us well in our career in music.

Gordon Lightfoot (see Figure 1.1) worked as a bank teller, a music copyist, a singer/dancer on a television variety show, and drove his dad's laundry truck in the small Ontario town where he grew up. Eliza

Gilkyson talks about some of her part-time jobs while she was writing songs, doing gigs, and raising a family:

> I answered telephones for an answering service from 10 P.M. at night until 6 A.M. in the morning. I had to feed my kids dinner, put them to bed, then drive over and answer phones until dawn, then come home and send the kids off to school.
>
> I was a gal Friday to my sister who was trying to help me figure out a way to support myself when I moved out to California. I was her assistant; she was a vice president at Warner Brothers in those days. I would work three or four hours a day a few days a week doing that.

I carried rugs in Boston, drove a taxicab in St. Louis, and did a little telemarketing in Omaha, Nebraska. We all do what we need to do to pay the bills, buy that better instrument, pay for that next recording, and hopefully move to the next level. In my experience in this business, few artists are given a free ride, and the ones who are don't seem to have the fire in their belly that you need to take the risks and do the hard work that is needed to succeed.

The best kinds of day jobs when you are moving forward as a singer/songwriter seem to be the ones that are associated somehow with your craft of music. These are also jobs that can keep you going when you hopefully segue into full-time status.

These sorts of jobs would be advertising jingle writing or singing, teaching guitar or some sort of music, working somehow in the media field as an independent producer, or working for a booking agency or record company in some capacity. Even though none of these may be closely related to the kind of music you are trying to write and/or perform yourself, the experience and knowledge you will gain from these sorts of jobs will serve you well as you transition to doing your music in a full-time manner, if that is what you aspire to achieve.

Dick Weissman talks about other opportunities for songwriters in a later chapter of this book.

Harry Manx worked in a Toronto blues club as a sound man, which is another one of those day (or in this case, night) jobs where you not only get paid but hopefully learn something about the life you hope to eventually be living yourself.

> The earliest memories were the drive to become a full-time musician, and that happened when I worked in a blues club in the early 1970s in Toronto, and I was mixing sound for John Hammond one night. I was a little too much into the sauce in those days, and

I remember saying to the manager the sound wasn't all it could be, to put it mildly. I ended up getting let go a few days later, so I decided I had had enough of being a sound technician and I decided I was going to be a musician, so I bought a ticket to Paris, showed up in Paris, and started performing on the streets by the next weekend. I think I was 19 at the time, and I declared myself then a musician, not a sound guy.

Of course, the reason you are working these kinds of day jobs is to write and perform your music. It is so important, when you are beginning to perform your own songs, that you take every opportunity presented to you to play the songs for people and make the all-important connections needed to get yourself heard.

This is definitely something to consider if you are contemplating a move to the songwriting centers of Nashville, New York, or Los Angeles. You may have some decent paying gigs where you are at right now, but you have to be aware that if you reside in any of the three aforementioned cities, your chances to make money playing your songs will virtually disappear when you are at home. For every gig that exists in those towns, there are hundreds of performing songwriters willing to play them for little or no pay, in hopes of getting their songs heard by a publishing or record company executive who will give them a break.

Music venues have taken advantage of this situation to provide free entertainment, much of it very good. Some clubs even require the artist to pay for a slot to perform his or her songs.

There are Cinderella stories where a move like this has worked out for the songwriter, such as in the cases of Randy Travis and Garth Brooks—but it is a long shot, and it is best to realize it as such and to have a contingency plan.

Full-Time Singer/Songwriter/Performers

This final general category is the group that many performing songwriters desire to be in, and it is one that requires constant attention to not only artistic output but also organizational and time-management skills.

This is a profession that offers tremendous fulfillment and freedom, but offers very little in the way of security. Although ASCAP, BMI, the Musicians' Union, and other organizations offer some reduced rates on health plans, basic health insurance is very expensive and often difficult to afford on a full-time musician's income. Unless you are frugal and wiser than most artists, retirement is a word that applies to other people, not to you.

The Musicians' Union is a viable organization, particularly active and powerful in major metropolitan areas such as New York and Toronto, Canada. They primarily bargain for symphony orchestra (and other larger musical organizations) wages and benefits, and offer health insurance and retirement benefits. However, a good part of those benefit contributions are agreed to by employers, and as an independent musician you are essentially self-employed. Some independent songwriter/performers will find membership in this organization useful to them; we will talk more extensively about the Musicians' Union in Chapter 3.

But at least when you are starting out and you make the jump to being a full-time professional singer/songwriter/performer (and probably for much of your career), plan on basically having to come up with benefits like health insurance and retirement yourself. There's an old joke about this:

Question: What do you call a musician without a girlfriend?
Answer: Homeless.

This scenario is more real than many artists would like to admit, unless they have planned and taken that part of their life very seriously.

As a full-time performing singer/songwriter, you need to not only become accomplished at your songwriting, but also:

- Learn what it takes to keep yourself booked on a consistent basis, be able to write a press release, put together an effective promotional package and Web site, and establish what your performance is worth in the marketplace.
- Run an effective office, keeping track of receipts and other information for tax purposes (you will be an independent contractor).
- Become adept at developing your own stagecraft, communicating with the audience, and providing not only your songs on stage but a complete presentation.

COPYRIGHTS FOR YOUR SONGS

Copyrights are actually a fairly simple concept. Like a patent, they establish ownership of your creative ideas, except they apply to intellectual property rather than inventions. The awarding of a copyright establishes authorship, ownership, publication, or transfer of a song, dramatic work, pictorial or sculptural work, motion picture, or sound recording.

When you write a song, technically you own the copyright. However, protecting it entails registering it with the Library of Congress. When you register the copyright, you are then eligible to sue anyone who infringes on your song not only for royalties but also for damages.

If you have not registered the song, you will have a more difficult time proving that your song was written before the one that you are claiming is copied from yours. You also will not be eligible to receive damages but only to receive appropriate royalty payments. If your song was written after 1978, it is automatically protected from its writing date until seventy years after the death of the last surviving author.

It will cost you $45 per song to have this protection of your work. You have to submit your application and a recording of each song to the Register of Copyrights, Library of Congress, Washington, D.C. 20559.

The easiest way to obtain the forms is from the Library of Congress Web site, which also has full instructions on how to fill them out and what kinds of recordings they accept.

The U.S. Library of Congress can be accessed at www.copyright. gov. There is a tremendous amount of information there to answer any questions you may have about the process.

When I first started applying for copyrights, only lead sheets were acceptable, and I used to toil over them for hours, trying to get the notation just right. Today you can send in almost any kind of reproduction (a CD, computer file, etc.) and it will be accepted for copyright purposes.

It is also possible to copyright an entire body of work, such as an album, for the one fee. This is a good temporary tactic if you are shopping your songs, but most artists and music lawyers agree that the protection of an individual work is not sufficient by doing this. If you place the song with a publisher, they will require you to copyright it (or do it themselves, and charge you for it later).

Techniques that friends may recommend that they have heard of, such as sending copies of your song to yourself with postmarks on the envelope, will not hold up in most courts of law, should you ever need to prove ownership of your song. Copyrighting an album's worth of original songs is a costly "extra" to recording an album, but a necessary step if you are serious about your songs and your career.

The book listed below (also shown in the bibliography) is an excellent source to answer any lingering questions you may have on copyrights that are unanswered or unclear to you on the copyright office Web site: Jeffrey and Todd Brabec, *Music, Money and Success: The Insider's Guide to Making Money in the Music Business,* 5th ed. (New York: Schirmer Trade Books, 2006).

PERFORMING RIGHTS ORGANIZATIONS (PROs)

This is how you get paid for your original compositions being played on radio, television, in the movies, and in any public performance situation.

In North America, the major PROs are ASCAP, BMI, SESAC, and CAPAC. Both writers and publishers belong to these organizations, which distribute the performance royalties that they collect to their members using a sampling system.

The two largest PROs are ASCAP (the American Society of Authors, Publishers, and Composers) and BMI (Broadcast Music Incorporated). Each of these organizations has a long and fascinating history, and they collect hundreds of millions of dollars a year that they distribute to their members. If you are making a living strictly as a songwriter, it's a PRO that mails you your major paychecks.

The debate is constant over which PRO is most magnanimous with its writers and publishers, and it truly depends on who you are, the kind of music you write, and what kind of a career you have. My good friend David Rea, who played lead guitar with Gordon Lightfoot and later with Ian and Sylvia, is also owner of 15 percent of the writer credit of Mountain's song "Mississippi Queen," which has had life as a radio hit, background music in commercials, and even in *The Simpsons* TV show. Over the years, Rea has received checks from ASCAP for that song totaling many thousands of dollars.

How did Rea wind up with the odd amount of 15 percent royalty on the song? He says,

> The drummer for Mountain and I basically wrote that song over a case of warm Shaeffer's beer in my old Toronto apartment. We showed it to Felix Pappallardi, and he and the other member of the group changed a couple of words, and for years I received 25 percent of the royalties. It was reassigned to 15 percent after a dispute about the actual percentages, but that is the way it goes sometimes. I am grateful it has provided me the income it has through the years, and that it continues to be used extensively on television and in movies.

The PROs all send quarterly statements out listing how your songs have been used and what media they have received airplay in. Those statements reflect the total royalty paid, then the percentage that you receive of that total.

Today, it costs nothing to join a PRO; you just have to establish somehow that one of your songs has been played on the radio somewhere, somehow, or performed in public.

I am a writer/publisher with ASCAP, and the principal reason I chose them is for their Special Awards program that gives out money each year, in addition to whatever quarterly royalty checks you may receive. ASCAP Special Awards program gives cash payments to artists

Figure 1.2 Eliza Gilkyson. Courtesy of Eliza Gilkyson and Val Denn Agency.

in styles of music that are not sampled adequately, such as folk, jazz, and blues. You fill out forms each year that detail where you have played, the radio play your music has gotten, the songs you have written, and so on. Somehow they come up with a figure they award you, paid annually in a lump sum. For me, it winds up being around a $1000 per year award, which certainly makes it worth belonging to ASCAP. BMI has no such program, though they have talked of instituting one in the near future.

Eliza Gilkyson (see Figure 1.2), on the other hand, has a strong reason for being with BMI. She says, "I am with BMI. My dad was with them his entire career as a songwriter, and I chose them for that reason. I did not even know there was another PRO at that time."

Gilkyson's songs are played often on adult acoustic alternative (AAA) radio format stations as well as public radio, and I'm sure BMI does a good job at helping her with her income stream. Years ago, ASCAP was unfriendly to blues, cowboy, and folk songwriters, and Gilkyson's dad was probably a BMI writer for that reason.

Each PRO has its own advantages and disadvantages, but it is important that you do some research and choose one to join.

2

FIRST STEPS, SONGS, AND GIGS IN BECOMING A WORKING COMPOSER/PERFORMER

FIRST PROFESSIONAL ENGAGEMENTS AND HOW PROFESSIONAL COMPOSER/ PERFORMERS OBTAINED THEM

Obtaining Those First Professional Engagements

- Research the club, concert series, or other venue in which you want to perform to ascertain if it is appropriate for you and your music.
- Make first contact via phone or e-mail.
- Send a promotional package and sample of your music.
- Follow up within one or two weeks to make sure the club owner received or has listened to the materials. Be polite and persistent if he or she has not done so, and continue to check back regularly until you get an answer.

The time-tested way of obtaining any paying engagement remains essentially the same since I began my career, with a few new twists. These elements are absolutely essential to this process.

Do your research and make sure the gig you are trying to obtain uses the kind of music you present. Occasionally you can buck a trend and convince the person making the entertainment decisions to try something different or new, but this is rare.

First, call and introduce yourself to the owner or booking agent for the venue, concert series, festival, or club; ask if you can send him or her a promotional package and recording. (This, in itself, is a great change over the process most commonly favored when I began to perform my songs. At that time, the most accepted way to get musical work was through a live audition. Today, requests by a venue booker for a live audition are uncommon, although there are many agents/bookers/owners who will not hire you until they see you in front of an audience.)

Do not waste your time or the time of the venue booker or owner until you have a promotional package/press kit or a Web site/shared site containing those materials (a shared site being an address like myspace.com).

Press Kits

The press kit should consist of:

- A biography of your musical career, including notable achievements or awards (such as in songwriting competitions), and other pertinent information.
- A page detailing recent appearances, emphasizing particularly prestigious venues or festivals.
- Reprints of positive press that has featured you or referred to your music. These can be from newspapers, Internet sites, even fan revues.
- If you have enough of these, put together a page of quotes from those various sources. Feature this page immediately after the venue listing page.
- If you have a festival organizer, club owner, or radio person willing to write a letter praising your songs and/or performance, ask him or her to give you one. This should be prominently featured in the package as well.
- An 8 × 10-inch glossy photo, suitable for use in a newspaper or other display.
- An 11 × 14-inch poster, with a photo of you or your most recent album, that has space for listing a time, date, and other information on your performance.

Today, all of this should also be posted on a well-designed and maintained Web site. If you do not have your own site, you can use a shared site such as myspace.com for free (though your bandwidth or availability for posting large files such as video will not be as great as if you have your own site). This is quickly becoming an essential promotional tool. On sites like hostbaby.com, you can even design and maintain your own Web site, with professional help and advice, for a nominal fee.

Do some research online or with other musicians you know who run and maintain their own sites to find out their recommendations. Today, Web sites can be hosted and maintained for as little as $20 per month, plus the annual fee for holding onto your domain name, generally less than $50 per year.

Regardless of your Web presence, you still need to have hard copies of promotional material to send. You will need to send a professional-sounding demo recording or album with the promotional material. You can submit a studio-produced CD, but most useful is a recording that is representative of how you will sound live in the venue, not just a CD with other instruments that tend to obscure or ornament your own sound and the sound of the song.

INSIGHTS FROM FEATURED SONGWRITERS AND OTHERS ON WRITING EARLY SONGS

There are many key differences in today's performing/composing world from the business as it existed when I began my career in the early 1970s.

Probably the greatest contrast between then and the brave new world of the early twenty-first century is in the ability to perfect your performing and composing in a situation that gave you "on the job" training, so to speak. Though many of the venues where a young songwriter could play were rough and required that you do other material in addition to your own compositions, you were paid to perform four or five sets a night, and you knew you could sneak some of your own songs in. Even in a place where the cigarette smoke was thick and the patrons were of questionable character, you could pretty quickly get a sense if a new song was working or not.

In 1974 I had a weeklong engagement at a pub in Canada that required five sets of music a night, five nights a week, and an additional three sets Saturday afternoon for what they called a "matinee." As I prepared to take the stage on the Saturday afternoon, I noticed that there was a phonograph set up on stage that had not been there when I had finished the night before. A few minutes later a very attractive young woman came up to me and asked if I was performing there, and proceeded to tell me she was appearing there that afternoon, too. I didn't think much about it at the time, but I noticed when I began my set that the audience consisted entirely of men. When I finished my set of cover hits and recent songs I had written, to resounding apathy, I was very surprised when the young woman who had spoken to me earlier came out and the phonograph began playing the song "Proud Mary." She proceeded to take off all of her clothes to a much different reception from the audience than the nonovation I had received a few minutes earlier. As soon as she was through dancing, I had to go up and play my songs again to a crowd that was, shall we say, less than enthusiastic to see me back up there. Still, I got paid, practiced my craft, and wrote new songs while I anticipated the next gig. In the 1970s, you could at least somewhat support yourself on the $40 to $75 you might make in a setting like that.

Today there are many fewer bars and restaurants that feature live music than there were thirty years ago. Some reasons for this include increased enforcement of venues paying ASCAP and BMI performing rights fees, the popularity of "sports" bars with many televisions, and the rise of karaoke as an alternative to live music. Changes in DUI laws and stricter enforcement of those laws have also had a negative impact on many venues' abilities to afford live music.

Consequently, it is much more difficult for the fledgling performer/ songwriter to get musical experience and reaction on whether an audience might appreciate his or her songs. If a bar/tavern/club/restaurant does have music and pays the performers, the pay is generally not much more for beginning musicians/writers/performers than it was in the 1970s.

Harry Manx says of his first paying gig, back in the 1970s,

> My first professional gig I was paid $125 and it was in a supermarket in Japan, and that was in the early eighties. The weird thing about it was, they put two of us on the stage at once—they had a clown and me. I asked, "Are you going to put both of us on stage at once?" They said, "Yes, that's our program today."

The return of the coffeehouse culture has provided many young songwriters with a first place to try out their music. Unfortunately, the vast majority of coffeehouses pay little or nothing to their performers, using them as an attraction to bring customers in or keep them there. Most composers playing in a coffeehouse make only the tips the customers put in their jar, and whatever money from CDs they can sell, if they have any available. Coauthor Dick Weissman even talks of a coffeehouse he discovered in Portland, Oregon, where you have to sign a contract acknowledging that you will not be paid!

The exception would be the nightclub/coffeehouse model that has a featured act that receives a substantial percentage of a cover charge at the door. Though most of these establishments book well-known composer/performers, many of them also have open-mike evenings where a beginning performer/songwriter can at least have a chance to play to an audience that is receptive to new musical works.

The performing songwriters of today, just beginning their journeys as an artist, have to look harder for venues to hone their craft. Many churches feature music both during the services and in concert settings away from worship services. There are many more festivals that feature music than existed thirty years ago, which is a plus. There are still clubs that pay performers well, but be aware the competition for these gigs will be fierce; prepare accordingly.

Most paying engagements available to beginning performers/composers today will be one-night stands. There are still a few places that hire pianists or guitarists who perform original music for multiple nights and multiple-week jobs, generally in hotels or resorts, but these have become less and less common. If you are fortunate enough to land a weeklong or multiple-night engagement in a club, you can expect performing fees to be in the $100 to $200 a night range for a solo artist, for a show that will require you to play three or four 45- to 60-minute sets of music.

Eliza Gilkyson remembers her first play-for-pay gigs in San Francisco, during the mid-1960s:

> The first time I got money, I passed the hat in Sproule Hall in Berkeley in 1969. I never did have a real day job for very long. I was a hippie, I lived in teepees, I lived in a tent one summer, I lived in an old wooden railroad boxcar that I paid $15 a month for . . . and many other interesting living situations to make this music happen.

My very first gigs were in a small lounge in Omaha, Nebraska, that was part of restaurant called the Golden Apple. It was a place that specialized in the then-very-hip fondue craze. I played 4 hours a night and received $35 for my trouble, and I loved every minute of it. The bartender was a crusty, small Italian guy by the name of Don, who had worked in the bar business his entire life. I learned more about life from talking to Don during my breaks than I ever learned from my brief (thankfully, for my teachers) sojourn in college. Every night that I walked into the Golden Apple to play, I felt privileged to play my songs and be paid for doing it.

Gordon Lightfoot had to go through the trials and tribulations we all have; he says, "I got the gigs just through telephoning and auditions at that time [when he began his career]. That was how things were done back then."

All of these decades later, when you first start out, you'll be getting those first gigs the same way.

If you are uncomfortable performing your songs solo and require other musicians to make the sound you desire, be aware that the pay you can ask for and receive will not increase commensurate to the number of people in the band. In Portland, Oregon, where I currently reside, there is a well-known chain of brew pubs, most of which hire music. They prefer duos and trios, but pay only a slight bit more than they pay for a solo: $150 on a Thursday night, $175 on a Friday or Saturday night.

This should be a good incentive to young composer/performers to become accomplished enough to present a complete, entertaining sound with one person, if possible. One of the drawbacks for young songwriters with respect to performance venues is that they are at the mercy of a buyer's market because of the limited options.

Eliza Gilkyson is convinced that it is essential to learn to create a compelling sound solo if you are to become a complete singer/songwriter, even if you eventually want to have a band accompany you:

> The guitar technique that I am known for comes from playing live. The best thing I think a songwriter can do is go out there and play those songs by yourself. I take the guys out with me on tour now, but to be able to accompany yourself comes from years of touring. The only way to really learn that skill is do to it solo.
>
> I had to learn ways of making that work and keeping it musical. I don't think of myself as a great guitar player at all, but I can certainly accompany myself well.
>
> I come up with little hooks, with little things that work for me. I probably couldn't sit down with anyone else's music and play anything of note, but I do know how [to] accompany myself. The single secret to accompanying yourself is a good grove, good time. A person who has a good sense of rhythm can get away with a lot.

I agree totally with Gilkyson's observations. Though I have a band that performs with me today in larger concert situations, there is nothing like the experience you gain when performing solo, when the total sound rests upon your ability. It is also where you learn your stagecraft—your ability to talk to an audience and to get them involved in what you are doing.

As riveting or as beautiful as your songs may be, oftentimes they need a short, coherent introduction to set them up for an audience. Some songwriters use humor to do this. Others use stories about how the songs came to be written and what they are about.

Overlong introductions are boring to the audience and detract from the flow of your presentation. At the other extreme, not communicating verbally at all to those listening to your music takes away a major reason for attending a live presentation, whether the listeners are hearing you in a bar, festival, or concert. People want a sense of who you are, and they want to be not only serenaded but also entertained.

There are a number of very successful professional singer/songwriter/performers who polished their audience skills by playing on the street for tips. It is hard for me to imagine a tougher gig that that, but lots of singer/songwriters who have done it are quite enamored of the experience. Bill Staines, the great New England songwriter, used to busk on the street with his good friend Jerry Rau from Minneapolis, who still loves playing for the folks walking by up in the Twin Cities. Rau has performed in concerts in Paris and on the popular *Prairie Home Companion* radio program with its peripatetic host, Garrison Keillor, but Rau still loves the vitality and uncertainty of the street-singing scene.

Harry Manx (see Figure 2.1) began playing professionally on the street in France, and has great stories about some of his early gigs on the sidewalks of some unusual locales, and the doors that it eventually opened for him:

When you play on the street, you really have to hold a crowd; they didn't buy a ticket to come in, there is no guarantee that you will make a penny. Unless you are really putting energy out, there is not much coming back you. That's a pretty serious life lesson, that you need to do a good job if you want to be taken care of that day. I learned not to be afraid to do a little shtick, to do whatever is needed to keep them happy. I'm not one of these guys who plays with his back to the crowd, or doesn't say anything to them. I want to engage my crowd; I want them to feel like the show is about them. That's what I try to give to them.

Once I was in Switzerland, and it was another dreary day of rain, and I really didn't want to be there on the street playing. But I did it anyway, and I started to get into it after a while. I look up, and I see this black guy leaning against the wall, watching me, and he was tapping his foot, kind of smiling, and he even came over and gave me a few bucks. I thought that was cool, kind of inspirational, so I packed my bags and I'm walking home past a club. I see that Dollar Brand [renowned South African keyboard player, who later changed his name to Ahmad Jimahl] is playing there, and I look at the picture, and I realize it's that same guy. What you're doing on the street, it might seem like it's not making a difference to anybody, but sometimes some people take notice.

So you never know who is there watching you. When I moved back to Vancouver, Canada, in 2000 I didn't know how to get in the music business. So I started again on the street, in Vancouver. A guy came along who is a producer, who has produced a number of decent bands in Canada. He stopped right away and said, "Oh no, not you, not here on the street. Here's my card, give me a call and I'll tell you what's up." So I gave him a call, and he passed me on to his wife, who went and got me a few gigs in clubs, and they just kind of pushed me into the business and said, "Go, go." I was very grateful for that.

Figure 2.1 Harry Manx. Photograph by Shari McDonald. Courtesy of Harry Manx.

The only way to become engaging at how you introduce your songs and involve your audience is by experimenting with your stagecraft and not being afraid to speak to the crowd listening to you.

Even at the beginning levels of your career, when you are performing your songs in a noisy bar and are convinced no one is listening, talk to the audience. Learn how to tell a good, concise story about the song. Tell them about how you wrote the song, or who the writer is and how or why you are singing it. Work in some humor. Play a song that the audience can sing along with, or somehow join with you by clapping in a certain spot. *Connect!* It is too easy to sit behind a guitar or piano and allow yourself to become background music. Sometimes that will happen despite your best efforts, but don't let it be because you didn't bother to try to communicate with those who are there.

When Harry Manx worked as a sound man in a Toronto, Canada, blues club, he was able to see some of the greats in that field do their shows. As he remembers, it wasn't just the music that set the crowd afire on the good nights, it was the way the performers worked the audience.

Watching those blues guys I realized that they had a lot of schtick going on—the way they dressed, the way they walked, the way they talked—and they used that style to hypnotize the people. Watching Buddy Guy and Junior Wells was amazing. My friend snuck me into this club when I was 15 and I watched those guys, and they were all dressed up in fur coats when they came in, with fedoras on their heads and girls on their arms, and they were dropped off by a Cadillac out front. They were doing that whole thing, and I loved the whole vibe around the scene.

Then when I saw Buddy Guy come off the stage with that long guitar cable, sit next to a girl, and order a drink, all while he was blowing a solo on his guitar, I thought, "Now, *this* is show business." I don't know how much musicality I got out of it, but I got a sense that you really have to find a deep groove.

Watching Muddy Waters just stay on one chord, and the band would be getting deeper and deeper into it, and just hypnotizing the people with that, so I saw that it wasn't so much about flashy technique as it was about digging into the groove as deep as you can, and once you got that going, people will get drawn into what you do. It taught me about focusing on the groove.

In a later chapter we will discuss the next level up performance-wise: small concerts, festivals, and special events. The pay scale can rise quite dramatically if you can work your way with your songs to that point. Interestingly enough, the better class of engagement you play, generally the more important it is that you are a composer of quality original music, which is something to keep in mind when the temptation is to become strictly a cover song act at the club level.

Eliza Gilkyson talks about booking herself, some of her experience in getting gigs early on, and the importance of getting out and performing on the road as soon as possible:

A couple of times I had some really nice promo packages, and I had several higher profile agencies that took me on. At the time I didn't really understand how important it was to tour. You really have to tour if you want to have a real career. It doesn't matter what level of success you are dealing with, if you don't tour, it is not going to happen. I never toured enough. I was raising a family and just couldn't figure out how to do it. I thought that if you just put out records, that was enough.

It wasn't until five or six years ago that I got an agent who said, "This is what you are going to have to do—get out there and eat it for a year." She said, "You are going to have to open for people who should be opening for you, and you are going to have to have a good attitude about it, because you are going to have to do that for one or two years." She also said, "Don't complain to me about it." I said, "OK, let's do it," because I realized that was the missing ingredient.

Sometimes in Austin, where I live, people get a really good local buzz. They get all heady with excitement about where their careers are going. But you get out on the road and twenty people show up in a place like Kansas City, because no one there knows who you are. That is the reality. That's what separates the girls from the women.

Of course, you can't get out on the road until you or that agent actually books the gig—so make sure you have your materials in place to get that done.

THE ROLE OF FORMAL MUSIC EDUCATION IN BEING A SUCCESSFUL COMPOSER

Many songwriters can read and write music, but probably even more songwriters don't possess these skills. Learning about music on a formal basis is simply a tool that will help you to communicate with musicians, music arrangers, record producers, and other songwriters. It also may introduce you to new musical styles, thereby increasing your versatility. This can enable you to write songs in a variety of musical genres, rather than restricting yourself to a single musical identity.

It is possible to study music on your own, with the aid of books and DVDs, but for most people taking classes is a quicker and more efficient way to approach it.

Formal music education does not automatically make one a good singer/songwriter/performer. It does, however, provide tools and basic knowledge that songwriters utilize as part of their bag of tricks when they compose. It is a little bit like trying to assemble a car with only a wrench, hammer, and screwdriver—it can probably be done, but it is going to be a tougher job.

On the other hand, songwriting is not only a craft, it is also art. As art, some of the best examples of it are almost totally intuitive. Paul McCartney has never been able to read or write music, yet has composed ballads that in many ways defined the last half of the twentieth century and seem destined to endure.

Still, I do not think Sir Paul would argue that at many points in his songwriting life, some basic knowledge of music theory would have made his work a little easier.

Harry Manx's music education was unorthodox, but clearly effective in its results:

> As a kid, I met guitar players and just kind of learned a lick here and there. The only formal training I had was when I was in India with Vishwa Mohan Bhatt, and I really did the whole Indian disciple thing where I showed up every morning, and I sat there on the floor in his house, in the music room, and he would give me a few things to get me started, a scale or something, and I would play for three or four hours. . . . That went on for many years.
>
> But otherwise, I still can't read music. I can read a chart if you put chords on there, but I can't read the notes in Western music. In Indian music, I can read it when it is written out.

There are a number of colleges that offer courses in songwriting, including short summer courses or intensive weekend workshops. For the songwriter looking to polish both theory and writing skills together, there are song schools that offer seven- to ten-day comprehensive tutorials at some of the major music festivals.

These typically have some professional performing songwriters who have been very successful, sharing their stories and working hands-on with you—someone like Steve Gillette, who wrote the oft-recorded song "Darcy Farrow," or Steve Seskin, who has written hits for country artists such as Kathy Mattea and Garth Brooks. Both of these songwriters are performers as well as writers, and regularly teach at the Kerrville (Texas) Folk Festival and Lyons (Colorado) Festival song schools. The curriculum consists of both lyric and melody writing tutorials, with small student-to-teacher ratios and lots of constructive criticism.

The tuition for these "songwriting camps" usually runs about $700 to $1000 per week. There are other opportunities for young and emerging performers to interact and trade songs with established masters too, at events like songwriter Tom Russell's yearly "SongTrain" excursions across Canada, which features artists like himself and Nanci Griffith at the mercy of aspiring songsmiths and fans who want to interact with them.

The bottom line seems to be that any education you can gain, from basic music theory to songwriting technique used by established artists, is bound to help you be a better writer yourself.

Gordon Lightfoot talks about the reason he sought a formal music education at Westlake School of Music in Los Angeles:

What I had learned about musical theory in public school and in high school was inadequate. Being at Westlake taught me to write in all of the keys, and that is what I really wanted to know. The piano keyboard was the basis of that whole course of study, which is what made it right for what I wanted to learn, bearing in mind that in 1960, all of the original lead sheets and arrangements were handwritten.

As it turned out, the skills he learned there would serve him again and again through the years—not only in writing his own songs but also in working as a music copyist to provide him with income while he was doing his early composing and performing, sight-singing in a dancing chorus on a CBC variety show, and later being able to voice the chordal structure he wanted to hear on the album arrangements of his compositions.

Later on in his career, when Gordon Lightfoot was able to hire a band for his concerts and live performances, that musical training proved valuable to him again:

I can give them [the band] the parts, which is one of the other reasons I took that Westlake course we talked about earlier. I can write the arrangements for the band, all of the parts, and I can write anything that I want to hear in any particular spot and then tell them to ad lib as they see fit. There are certain places they have to do it the way I want it done, but in between they can make it up as they go.

They add a lot to the arrangements. They just have certain cues, and the rest of it they can just wing it. They have their chord sheet in front of them with cues on it when they first learn the song.

I was in a university music education course of study, but I was always more interested in writing, playing, and performing the music (and meeting girls while I did that) than I was in mastering the secrets of counterpoint and writing in all of the keys, and I quit after a short period of time. Coauthor Dick Weissman has put his formal music skills to good use as an arranger, producer, and studio musician, which has helped him pursue his lifelong love affair with the banjo. In retrospect, I wish I had gained more basic musical knowledge. I can write a lead sheet, and have some basic theory on board, but my musical journey might have been a little less bumpy with more navigational tools.

Eliza Gilkyson talks about her own experience with formal musical training:

I don't have formal musical training, and on the piano I am self-taught. I am in the process of having my songs transcribed for sheet music now.

On a CD like *Redemption Road,* I wrote a very complex orchestrated piece called "Through the Glass Darkly," in which I was playing almost everything, and then I composed parts for flutes and other instruments—but I had to sing them their parts.

SONGWRITING INFLUENCES AND THE IMPORTANCE OF TRADITIONAL MUSIC AND MELODY

There are two distinct schools of thought on the importance of influences in songwriting. Some successful songwriters I have known prefer to listen to no one in their field, preferring to concentrate totally on their own writing experience. If they listen to other music, it is outside their own genre or incidental (such as hearing others perform at a festival). They feel that approaching their music in this fashion gives them a chance of creating something new and fresh.

Others, and I count myself among this number, are very aware of what other songwriters are creating, and are fans of the music as well as writers. This approach gives you a basic appreciation and knowledge of the style of music you are working at. It also has the advantage of drawing you into the musical community that you aspire to be a part of.

Even if you do not listen to anything contemporary in your chosen field, I believe it is imperative to know the background and basic roots of the music you are trying to write yourself.

For example, if you are working on writing a blues/rock-and-roll–oriented song, don't just listen to the Rolling Stones or Led Zeppelin; go back and listen to the people who influenced them and gave them their inspiration, the true originators of the form. Bluesmen like Howling Wolf, Skip James, and Robert Johnson are very accessible to everyone now via widely distributed recordings and the Internet.

I wish I could count how many times I have had songwriters/performers canvass me and ask to be on the radio show or to be hired to play a festival I direct. When I have listened to their tape or CD, if I have rejected them because I think they are not ready for that step, they often ask me what they can do to improve their material. I, in turn, ask them who they are listening to and influenced by, and if they are acoustic musicians, often times the answer is Neil Young or the Indigo Girls.

While listening to your musical heroes is inspirational and motivational, to truly become a masterful songwriter/performer yourself it is important to go back to get a grasp on some of the traditional forms that inspired those heroes.

In the 1960s, Gordon Lightfoot and his lead guitarist, Red Shea, spent a number of late nights listening repeatedly to an album Don Gibson recorded, "Songs of Stephen Foster," the great nineteenth-century American writer who wrote "My Old Kentucky Home," "I Dream of Jeanie with the Light Brown Hair," and many other classics. Lightfoot remembers,

> He and I got into the Stephen Foster idea by listening to a Don Gibson album [an early 1960s country artist], where he did all Stephen Foster songs. He did several hip, country versions of a lot of those old songs and made a beautiful album. Red and I got piped into that and we got thinking about Stephen Foster—that's how I really got interested.
>
> Red and I got into a Stephen Foster kick there for about a year, and I got all of that into one of my songs called "Your Love's Return" on the *If You Could Read My Mind* album.

When I asked Lightfoot subsequently where he thought his exquisite melody sense came from, which is one of the hallmarks of his songs, he said, "I'm not too sure where that comes from. I don't know if anybody really is. I can only remember that it started very, very young."

As a young songwriter, Lightfoot was very influenced by the artists he encountered in the clubs of Toronto—artists like Ian and Sylvia, who went on to become personal and professional friends, and Bob Gibson, who inspired both Lightfoot's 12-string guitar technique and his use of song structure.

> Bob Gibson was a wonderful folk artist, and great musician and teacher. He was a great friend, and I loved his music. I think he loved mine, too.
>
> He did a great performance with the 12-string or 5-string banjo. He played the 5-string banjo in a unique fashion, not in a bluegrass way, but in a more ethereal style. Watching him play and tune the 12-string guitar gave me a challenge to match the intonation of that guitar. I've been trying to match that intonation all my life, from remembering the sound of Bob Gibson's 12-string.
>
> A lot of his songs had a great historical significance to them. He sang and wrote wonderful songs, like the "Civil War Trilogy."

If you are writing melodically based music like Gordon Lightfoot or Bob Gibson, it would serve you well to listen to some of the timeless melodies that have been passed on through the ages by thousands of performers. These tunes are still recorded on many Celtic and other traditionally based albums, and writing melodies without having heard them is akin to tying one arm behind your back and trying to climb a mountain, particularly if you are hoping your songs will last beyond your own lifetime.

Become familiar with the Chieftains, Ira Gershwin, Woody Guthrie, Stephen Foster, Robert Johnson, and dozens of other important influences cited by people you admire as songwriters, and you will be the better artist for it. Learn some of these artists' interpretations of those old songs, and become part of the great music tradition of the human race, a warm blood flow that has persisted for centuries with no thanks to record companies, promotional budgets, or anything else except the magic of the melody.

One of the most difficult things to do is to write a simple, catchy melody, yet nothing else in music is more memorable. Meanings of words, sentence structure, and language are constantly changing, yet the power of a melody to affect the human heart and spirit seems timeless. Witness the themes of Beethoven, Mozart, Brahms, and Bach in their greatest works, many of which utilize very simple lines that cross both generational, time, and geographical boundaries to remain some of the most distinguishable musical pieces on Earth today, centuries after their composition.

So, don't shortchange your melodies behind three "good enough" chords that hold up three verses, three choruses, and a bridge. Make yourself familiar with what songwriting tools and structure work for the songwriters you admire, and educate yourself on the traditional music that is a key to music's boundless appeal.

I have always found it interesting to know what kind of prose and poetry writing songwriters who appear on *River City Folk* enjoy reading, and I have had some surprising answers through the years. Just like writing a melody, I think it is important for a lyric writer to appreciate and be familiar with some of the masters of the language we are working with.

Harry Manx is very poetic in his songs, and writes many of his lyrics with an underpinning of spirituality. Asked about those influences, Harry said,

> I had a real thing for poetry when I was a kid. When I left my home I took two Dylan Thomas books, and even at fifteen, they meant

a lot to me. I couldn't really understand it, I just felt something about it. This was long before I heard that Bob Dylan was into Dylan Thomas. I also had a book from the English poet Browning, whom I liked a lot.

Later on in life I came to be more interested in mystical poetry: Kahlil Gibran, Tigor [a great Indian poet], and Rumi. I really enjoyed poetry that also had a spiritual base to it.

I believe it is much more difficult to be an accomplished songwriter and create a body of work that you will be proud of if you are not also a reader. Reading has been a constant source of inspiration through the years to me, not only for subject matter but also for form, syntax, and structure. One of my best known songs, "The Boardwalk at Skagway," was inspired by the writing of Jack London, who captured in his incisive prose the excitement of the last great adventure on the American frontier, the Klondike Gold Rush. I had gone back and read Jack London's work again because of a fine tribute song to him by my great friend and fine Wyoming songwriter, Chris Kennedy. I went on to record Kennedy's "Jack London" song later, and I have been fortunate to perform in Skagway, Alaska, many times because of performing those songs.

Eliza Gilkyson is known for her succinct, concise portrayals of people and political situations. Certainly, one of the hardest things to do is to write a nonpreachy political commentary song, but she seems to be very adept at it. She also uses elements of the romance poets in her sparse phrasing, of which she says,

> I love William Butler Yeats, because he suggests, then builds, towards a passion and release that I relate to. In that sense, I am influenced by him but I am not a real studied writer that way. Songwriting has always been an emotional, cathartic experience for me.
>
> I used to be way too wordy, overlong, and self-indulgent in my explanations and I have just had to learn to economize in that way, that less is more. What I try to do is give people enough imagery, without too many words. The real art is [to use] just enough imagery so that listeners can then create their own images, and that's what hooks people. That is how people travel along with you, by you triggering their own imagination.
>
> I think if you give too much information it is like watching television, where your imagination becomes passive. I think that is what separates good writing from the other kind.

Eliza Gilkyson also had the good fortune to grow up with a father who was a full-time working singer/songwriter and performer. Terry Gilkyson had many songs featured in movies and the new medium of his day, television, and he also performed live solo and with various bands through the years. He received an Oscar nomination in the Best Song in a Movie category for his composition "The Bare Necessities" from Walt Disney's movie *The Jungle Book.*

She talks about her dad and both the positive and negative influences of growing up with a professional songwriter as her father:

> More than anything he sat me down and taught me, it was just that his music was around me in an absorbing fashion in so many different ways. He was so musical himself, and his melodies just permeated our lives. He had a feel for the dark, emotional melodies, but he could also be playful. His sense of chord progression and song structure, melody, they all became my paradigm. Then there were his friends, and his bands. There were the Easy Riders, but then also friends like VanDyke Parks, and guys that went on to sing and perform with Ry Cooder. I was utterly entranced by these people. They were like rock stars to me, but they were real, and in our home. That's who I listened to . . . who my dad knew. I never even discovered someone like Woody Guthrie until later, because I was totally into my dad's scene.
>
> My dad was an incredibly sensitive guy. I think he just became overwhelmed by the circumstances of his life. He moved to Santa Fe, and just kind of checked out.

As singer/songwriters/performers, we all have our share of disappointments, and it is sometimes hard for us to see the forest for the trees, even for an artist as successful and gifted as Terry Gilkyson was. Eliza talks about what it was like to see him go through some of those times, and what she learned from it that has helped her in her own career:

> He was not a self-esteem builder, by any means, because he had his own issues of self-acceptance. I think that is something that gets passed on to children. Later on, I think he did voice a lot more support. . . . He would say, "I don't know how you guys do it," and he let us know he was proud of us.
>
> One of my biggest memories is going to the Academy Awards with my dad. He was up for the best song award for the song "The Bare Necessities," from the Disney movie *Jungle Book.* He took me as his date, and we were in the front row. Louis Armstrong came out and sang his song, and it was by far the most fabulous song. . . . I

think it was actually Louis Armstrong's last public performance. But [my dad's] song did not win. The song that won was "I Talk to the Animals." Which song do *you* remember?

I felt that moment of tension sweep over him, that he had prepared for, and felt his disappointment. That night we got in the VW van and drove to New Mexico from L.A. I think that is where he turned his back and left.

What was amazing was, he didn't see that he had made it all the way to the world stage with that song, and gotten an Academy Award nomination. That is more than a Grammy, that is like the ultimate recognition, just to get the nomination. The actual winning of it is very much politics.

I remembered that circumstance when I got my Grammy nomination last year. I remembered that white heat that moves through your body just before your name is called . . . or not. Then that sense of disappointment when you don't get it . . . you almost feel embarrassed.

My dad took things way too personally. I take things personally too, but I know it's best not to. I think in a lot of ways I have better tools for taking care of myself in the way of being an artist, because to be an artist you have to be receptive, and you have to stay vulnerable to everything that is going on around you. You work off of that to create, but at the same time, life can be brutal and painful and you are this open, sentient person who is getting whumped upside the head. You have to learn ways of protecting yourself and taking care of yourself if you really want to be an artist for the rest of your life and not fall prey to indulgence and anesthetization.

You have to surround yourself with people who love you and tell you the truth, who have nothing to do with your career. You have to have a personal life that, in a way, has nothing to do with your career.

Musically, Eliza Gilkyson's first and probably her most important life influence was her dad and his music. She also was very affected by the psychedelic scene going on in San Francisco in her youth:

I was into Moby Grape, Jim Morrison, and Buffalo Springfield, Quicksilver Messenger Service, and Spirit. I *loved* the group Spirit. I was in a relationship with Mark Andes for 5 years, who was the bass player in Spirit, many years later.

For Harry Manx, he started out a lifelong love affair with the blues first listening to albums, then mixing sound for some of the legends he had heard on record, and then beginning to emulate those sounds:

First would be Muddy Waters, especially his acoustic album, which was called *Folk Music,* with Willie Dixon and Buddy Guy, all playing acoustic.

I was more attracted to Chicago blues, though I really don't play much of that. I always listened a lot to Buddy Guy and Junior Wells. I was a huge fan of Johnny Winters and his slide playing; I think he is a great player.

J. J. Cale is another influence of mine. I missed the whole Stevie Ray Vaughan thing, I was already gone when he got famous. Stevie Ray sounds to me like Albert King, who I was really into when I was a kid.

I mixed sound for Hound Dog Taylor at the club once. He was amazing—very raw, really a driving blues.

After growing up in a nonmusical household, I devoured everything I could listen to, from Brahms's *First Piano Concerto,* to sitting in the basement trying to figure out Chet Atkins finger-style arrangements, to Ian and Sylvia singing French folk songs. As I progressed in my career, I continually learned and was inspired by other writers attempting to do the same thing I was trying to do myself: compose good songs, sing them for people who wanted to hear them, and make a living somehow by doing that.

Many of my musical *compadres* in those days are well known now, but many of them gave up the fight and transitioned into more secure ways to feed themselves and put a roof over their heads. Nonetheless, I am just as grateful to great performing singer/songwriters but relatively unknowns—like Peter Mathieson from Toronto, Mark Moebeck from St. Louis, Bernie McDonald from the Missouri Ozarks, and too many others to mention—as I am to the artist friends who found a way to make every dream they ever sang a reality.

MAKING THE DECISION TO BECOME A FULL-TIME PERFORMING SINGER/SONGWRITER

It has been estimated than well over 90 percent of the performing singer/songwriter/musicians in this country are part time—that is, the money they make from those activities is the smallest part of their income.

It is an incredibly demanding task to become self-sufficient using your music as your sole support. At least initially, and in many cases for the rest of your life, you have to not only write good songs and perform them well with a good stage presence, but you also have to be booking agent, publicist, travel agent, accountant, and professional driver.

These tasks require hours and hours of time and dedication, aside from the music. Whereas a full-time day job might demand 49 or 50 hours per week, this profession is going to ask much more of you than that, if you are to be successful.

Again, there are two distinct schools of thought when it comes to becoming a full-time performing singer/songwriter, and your decision which one to follow greatly depends on your confidence, comfort level, and responsibilities.

One theory is that you will never really do completely what is needed to be done until you cast yourself adrift from the day job and have the time to concentrate on your music—as well as the terror of bill collectors—to inspire you to accomplish the other tasks I described.

The second approach is that you continue to work one or more day jobs, finding employers that will be adaptable to your performance schedule and eventual travel requirements, until you reach a point of such success that you have to decide on either the job or the musical career.

Both schools of thought are valid, and only you can decide which is best for your lifestyle and aspirations.

Gordon Lightfoot met Ian and Sylvia in 1961 at the First Floor Club in Toronto, before any of them had become well known, and eventually they gave him a "hand up the ladder." After Peter, Paul, and Mary heard Ian and Sylvia's version of the Lightfoot song "For Lovin' Me," Peter, Paul, and Mary also recorded it. Peter, Paul, and Mary's manager, the legendary Albert Grossman (who also was Bob Dylan and Ian and Sylvia's manager) and his partner John Court traveled to Toronto to catch Gordon performing live at the Purple Onion. Gordon says,

> That's how I got the United Artists record contract. That is why Albert Grossman and John Court came to Toronto to see me. That's why we are having this conversation, that is what happened. Peter Yarrow arranged the song, and it went up to #5 on the Billboard chart. They got the song through Ian and Sylvia, who were the first to record it.

He was still working a day job at that time, but that visit from Grossman and Court would change his life. When I asked him what was the point he knew he could do his music for a living, he said,

When I was about twenty-four years of age, and Albert Grossman and John Court came into the picture. I was nervous because I was reluctant to sign their contract. I was having second thoughts about whether to sign the contract. Anyway, I had no idea of the importance of it; it did not register. I was too young, and too inexperienced to understand that these people could make record deals in the U.S. with major record companies.

I got piped in right at the very beginning; I had no idea that I would wind up going into that office [Albert Grossman and John Court's office] in 1964 and wind up having Dylan as a stablemate. I got to meet Dylan, and got to know him a little bit. It was just a very interesting stretch of time through there.

I didn't have any hit singles for a number of years, but I was making all those albums, writing, and always had a good crowd to come see us. Album artists were really very popular back in those days, and you didn't need a hit for your reputation to go before you.

There was a great advantage in the Grossman organization in just being part of it. There was the aura of Peter, Paul, and Mary, Bob Dylan, Ian and Sylvia, and Odetta. Odetta was great too. She wasn't as much of a celebrity as were the others, but she was still great. Dylan was huge; he was as big as the Beatles at that point.

That was the end of Lightfoot's chapter in his life where we worked day jobs, then hustled off to do the nighttime gigs. However, he still talks fondly about those times and the various jobs he had to do to get to that next level.

Most of the first songs that any of us have written are thankfully forgotten or filed away in some dusty attic. There are some notable exceptions to that rule, however.

Ian Tyson's first song attempt was written in a hospital bed when he was recovering from a rodeo mishap. That song was "Four Strong Winds," which has been recorded by literally hundreds of folks since Ian penned it.

However, when you have written that first song that lights up the eyes of your audience and you can feel the response from them in your bones—that is an incredible boost to your confidence. For Lightfoot, those early songs of his—"For Lovin Me" and "Early Morning Rain"— would change his life forever. Harry Manx has a clear memory of the first good song he knew he had written:

It was a song called "Coat of Mail." The funny thing is, I wrote the song in about 5 minutes, and it was almost like I was channeling it; I just had to pick up the pen, and there was the song. But it was because I met a man I hadn't seen in so long, 25 years, and I met him on the street, he was a homeless guy. He was standing there with his hat in his hand right in front of me. It shocked me and it moved me so much I just went home and knew I had to write about it, and I wrote that song about him. I learned from that experience it is all about motivation, and if you are motivated, the song comes pretty quick and pretty easy.

3

WHERE DO I GO FROM HERE?

Getting Your Songs Heard ... On Stage and Beyond

PERFORMING USING YOUR ORIGINAL COMPOSITIONS

The single most important method of getting your songs heard should be obvious. The songwriter/performer simply needs to play them, sing them, and polish them every chance he or she gets.

This includes family get-togethers, open mikes, and paid gigs; every time you perform the song live, there is a potential booking agent in the audience or someone who may be interested in recording your song.

There are effective organizations, such as TAXI (which is talked about in detail in Chapter 8), that will promote your song(s) to producers, ad companies, and record companies for a set fee. This has worked for a few artists, but has also left many songwriters disappointed in their results. Like every other part of this business, it is a crapshoot—but one that you can increase your odds of winning exponentially by playing your music every chance you get.

Performer/songwriters can never be sure when someone is there who can do them some good, and sometimes that positive outcome can take years. I did a concert in Sitka, Alaska, for a radio station in 1993, and after the concert I met an agent who booked concert tours in Alaska, the Yukon, and British Columbia each winter. He expressed interest in my show and songs, we talked vaguely in terms of price for the tour (ten concerts, around $700 per show, plus CD sales, plus all travel, lodging, and meal expenses). I followed up the contact by both mail and phone, but I did not hear back from him.

Four years later I was passing though Cody, Wyoming, on a Monday night. A friend of mine had helped set up a small gig there that perhaps forty people attended. I had been on the fence all day about whether to do the gig or not, but decided I should, and make good use of my time there. Lo and behold, who should be at that show (by total coincidence) but Frank Howes, that Alaska agent who had talked to me in Sitka years before. He offered me that next Alaska/Yukon/Canada tour that night, and we signed the contracts the next morning at the Irma Hotel in Cody.

Had I decided not to go to Sitka to play a marginally profitable gig, I would not have met that agent. Had I decided not to play in Cody for what I knew would be very small crowd on a Monday night, I would not have made contact with him again, and most certainly the tour would have gone to someone else. The tour wound up being not only profitable but also a great journey that took me as far north as Yellowknife, Northwest Territories, a place I doubt I will perform at or see again in my lifetime.

Similar series of events have occurred many times during my career, and such are connections made in the music business.

When in doubt about doing a gig, always err on the side of playing your music, rather than loafing at home or sitting in the motel room and watching TV. Following this course of action will ultimately pay much greater dividends than the pay from the gig, whether those dividends be monetary or otherwise. Do bear in mind, however, that those dividends may not be immediately apparent.

Terry Currier wears three hats: he is the head of one of the most successful independent music stores in the United States, Music Millennium, in Portland Oregon; he is owner of his own record company, Burnside Records; and he is a partner in a national album distributor, Burnside Records Distribution. Terry has this to say about the importance of an artist doing any gigs he or she can obtain:

> Artists need to be as visible as they can possibly be. It depends on the artist, and it depends upon their music. If you were a singer/ songwriter in Portland, I would look for every opportunity you have to play to a large group of people, by trying to be an opening act for an established national act. If you know you have an opportunity to do that, and your music is in the vein of the headliner's music, that is the best audience you could play for.

You're not always going to get those chances, so you have to go out and play for the crowds of twenty and twenty-five people, too. You need to get in front of people that you think are going to appreciate your music and embrace it.

Kelly Joe Phelps, my Burnside Records artist, played 400 gigs a year for two years in a row, from his Portland/Vancouver base. Some of those places were clubs where he just got paid, and the music was an afterthought and the drinks and food were the first thought.

Still, he played 800 gigs in 730 days, and all of a sudden everything connected. I'm not saying that everyone needs to go to those lengths, but really, you have to go to establish some credibility within the artist's community in your town.

CONTRACTS

A wise man once told me there was no reason for a club owner or concert promoter to balk at signing a contract, unless he or she was planning on breaking it.

That being said, if you achieve any degree of success as a working performing singer/songwriter, you will probably be going back and doing repeat gigs and festivals. Personal relationships are what this business is all about—but to protect you and the owner, director, or promoter, it is always best to have something on paper.

If you are a member of the Musicians' Union, it is possible to use their contracts in dealing with clubs or other clients. These are relatively simple forms that specify the date and time of the engagement and when payment will be made for your services. The union will guarantee payment of the contract, initially paying you union minimum wages, and later suing the client to get any monies that are more than the union minimums. Some venues will not agree to using union contracts because they are opposed to unions in general, or the Musicians' Union in particular.

I work frequently at an Irish pub in Portland, Oregon, where the owner asks me how much he owes me after the biggest Irish festival on the West Coast is completed every year. That is the way he likes to do things, and he and I have a business relationship that stretches back sixteen years. In my initial dealings with him, however, I did have a signed contract.

Here is the all-purpose contract I use these days for my music performance dates, which is actually quite a bit more detailed than the standard Musicians' Union contract.

Tom May Concert Tours

Vignette Productions/Blue Vignette Publishing ASCAP
ADDRESS
www.tommayfolk.com

Contract for Performance Services

This Contract made this ___ day of _____, 20___, by _____ for _____
_____ (referred to as Employer) and Tom May/
Vignette Productions (referred to as Artist).

Artist agrees to supply musical entertainment at _____ on
_____. Artist will provide _____ sets of musical entertainment on each of the afore-
mentioned dates. Each set will consist of _____
_____ and begin at _____. Breaks shall be _____ and end at
_____.

Employer agrees to pay Tom May the sum of _____ for each of the above-mentioned
dates. Payment will be made ___ by check ___ by cash no later than _____. In
some situations, a deposit guarantee is required. If so, this amount is ___ to be mailed to the
above address by _____.

If Tom May's band is engaged, he may request that the amount be divided into individual
checks for himself and the other musicians.

It is understood that this contract is binding on both parties. It cannot be canceled except as fol-
lows: Artist and employer mutually agree that either party may cancel this contract or all parties
shall be released from all damages or liability thereunder, if and only if the Artist or Employer is
unable to fulfill the terms of this contract due to an act of God or any other legitimate condition
beyond the control of the Artist and Employer. However, it is agreed that "best efforts" will be
made by all to adapt so that the program may be presented as scheduled. If the Employer fails
to uphold any condition of this contract, the Artist may cancel the performance without releasing the Employer from the obligation to pay in full the agreed-upon wage.

Technical Requirements

The Employer is responsible for providing the following checked items ___ stage or elevation; ___
dressing room(s); ___ appropriate stage lighting; ___ a PA system, which shall include ___ microphones and microphone stands. In addition to main speakers, ___ monitors will be provided.

Other required technical notes: _____
_____
_____.

Note: Unchecked items are either not applicable or are the responsibility of Tom May.

Overnight accommodations for ___ people for ___ nights will be provided at no cost to the Artist. ___ meals will also be provided at _____.

Artist agrees to arrive at _____ for setup and sound check. Artist shall be allowed to sell
CDs and announce upcoming performances

If the event is outdoors and cancelled due to weather conditions, the Employer agrees to pay the
Artist ___% of the agreed-upon wage on the aforementioned date of payment. The Artist will try
to reschedule, but inability to do so shall not release the Employer from payment of wage on the
aforementioned date.

Artist agrees to supply promotional material in a timely manner and to list the event on his
website, if desired.

Signature: Employer   Signature: Tom May

_____   _____

Please sign both copies and return one to: _____

Figure 3.1

This covers most of the basic agreement points for a performance contract. You can amend it as needed for your own purposes.

Many performers also attach riders for certain situations, such as specific dietary requirements, no animals if a home stay is provided for, and so forth.

SONGWRITERS' ASSOCIATIONS

Many larger communities today have songwriters' associations that get together once a month or more often and share songs among members. Typically at these gatherings each member will perform a song and the other attendees will critique it.

These organizations are also clearinghouses for information about song markets and offer many resources, particularly to the beginning songwriter.

Most of them also produce one or more showcases, open to the public, which provide the songwriter with a chance to perform his or her music in public. Unfortunately, these showcases rarely pay the chosen performers, but they are an opportunity to get your songs heard.

They also typically offer workshops with established singer/songwriters to give their membership a chance to experience a working writer's knowledge firsthand. These workshops can be valuable, and usually run about $25 to $50 depending on the songwriter giving the seminar.

There is no central clearinghouse or umbrella organization for songwriting associations. You can generally find out what is available in your area through either an Internet search or inquiries at local music stores.

The most significant of the many local and regional songwriting organizations is the Nashville Songwriters Association International (NSAI). They have offices in Nashville, provide valuable networking opportunities for members who live or work there, and hold frequent classes and seminars with high-level professional songwriters and publishers. Since Nashville probably has more nonperforming professional songwriters than any of the other music business centers, this organization can provide you with many valuable contacts if you plan to move to Nashville or if you spend enough time there on a regular basis to pursue musical opportunities there.

Seminars such as the ones offered by songwriters' associations are also offered at many music stores, with subjects covered such as songwriting, guitar technique, stagecraft, equipment use, and so on. Some manufacturers such as Peavey sponsor these workshops in hopes they will generate sales for their products. Again, inquiries at the music stores you frequent will generally give you information on workshops in your area.

THE MUSICIANS' UNION/AFTRA/OTHER PROFESSIONAL ORGANIZATIONS

For singers and instrumentalists, there are two unions that deal with the music industry. Singers who do not play musical instruments are covered by AFTRA (American Federation of Television and Radio Artists), and AFM (American Federation of Musicians) deals with musicians. If you are a singer who plays a musical instrument, usually you would join the AFM—although should you do television work or sing on commercials, you will also need to join AFTRA.

Benefits of Joining a Union

We will now deal with the question of whether it is advantageous for you to join the union. If you get to record for a major label—by which we mean Sony, BMG, Capitol, Universal, or Warner Music—the decision has already been made for you. Their agreements with AFM and AFTRA require you to join one of these unions. By the same token, they are required to pay you a minimum set by the union, referred to as scale, for playing or singing on the recording sessions. Typically these companies will agree to consider each song as a separate recording session, whether you get it down in 30 minutes or 30 days. Between the union minimum payment, which is currently about $350, the 10 percent set-aside for your session, and $19 for health and welfare payments, you will actually gross about $400 for each song.

Some independent labels are signatories to union agreements and some are not, so this is something you are definitely going to need to know before you sign the contract. Joining AFM will cost you a minimum of $100 in a medium-size local, and two or three times that amount in the largest local. There are also quarterly dues that again vary from local to local, and also work dues. Work dues are a sort of tax on the working musician, ranging from 2 to 3 percent of the union minimum wage on all jobs. Some locals have a cap on work dues, which means that in Portland, Oregon, for example, work dues cost no more than $40 a year.

The disadvantage of union membership is obvious: you will have to pay an initiation fee, and then additional dues and work dues to maintain your membership. There are a number of benefits of being a union member, which may or may not be appropriate for your particular situation. They include:

- Guaranteed contracts.
- A pension plan.
- Access to jobs that come through the union.

- Discounts, ranging from recording studio time to the purchase of musical supplies.
- Residual payments for working on commercials, and Special Payments Fund income for playing on recordings.
- Jobs can be obtained through the Music Performance Fund.
- Reuse payments if a recording is used in other media—for example, if a recording is used in a movie or on a commercial.
- Free rehearsal space (not all union locals have rehearsal spaces).

Under the guaranteed contract clause, if you file a union contract and the employer does not pay you, the union will pay you the union minimum immediately. If you have been hired at a rate above the minimum wage, the union will take the employer to court; if and when they win the case, the union will pay you the additional amount above the union minimum.

The pension plan requires that you earn $3000 a year through union contracts for a period of five years. It will pay you about $2.55 a month at age sixty-five for each $100 contributed to the fund. If you are a full-time professional, this is a valuable tool, and over the years the amount will add up. There is also disability protection if you become injured or ill and can no longer play. It is also possible to take the pension at age fifty-five, but it pays considerably less if you do so.

The residuals paid to singers on commercials or voice-over talent by AFTRA can be enormous, as much as six figures for a single major product. Musicians get considerably less, but if you do enough different products, that amount can be considerable as well. My coauthor, Dick Weissman, has earned as much as over $2000 in residuals from playing on an hour-long airline commercial.

The Special Payments Fund pays bonuses to all musicians who play on recordings that utilize union contracts, based on the sale of *all* records, not the ones that you personally played on. A similar fund exists for people who play on films, although the payments for that fund are based on the gross of the particular film that you played on. AFTRA has bonus payments for singers who have performed on hit records, based on various sales plateaus.

The Music Performance Fund also comes from the sales of recordings. The money is used to pay musicians who perform free concerts at schools, nursing homes, and malls.

When Not to Join the Union

If you produce your own records and negotiate your own contracts with people whom you know, if you are a pure songwriter who never or rarely performs, or if you never work outside of a specific area, you may not find it economically feasible to join the union. Many club owners refuse to sign union contracts, but remember that if you do not have a union contract, then the union will not guarantee payment for the gig.

Each musician needs to evaluate his career in terms of where he is actually working and what his ultimate objectives are. Over the years, both Dick Weissman and I have witnessed a number of union officials who seemed to have no interest in anything but swing music or the symphony, for example. Weissman has even seen the president of a local insulting a country musician, telling him that he didn't play real music. By joining the union, you will meet many professional musicians who run the gamut of musical styles, and you may find this stimulating or annoying, depending upon your own preferences and prejudices.

Most union locals require that you reside in the geographic area where the local is located. However, there is a relatively new local of the AFM called Local 1000, known informally as the traveling folksinger's union. This local accepts contracts from all over the United States and Canada, and makes life a bit easier for the touring musician. Ordinarily, as a member of a particular local, you are required to file contracts at each local whose territory you are performing in. This can be quite a nuisance, so the traveling local is an interesting innovation.

Over the past ten years, a number of union locals have become a source of employment through e-mails, Web sites, and phone calls. Some have even actively gone into the business of booking musicians. Depending upon your objectives and the policies of a particular local, you may be able to utilize these contacts as a source of gigs.

NARAS

NARAS is the National Academy of Recording Arts and Sciences, best known as the group that is responsible for the Grammy awards. During the past fifteen years or so, the organization has expanded into many new regional chapter offices. The current lineup includes New York, Philadelphia, Washington, D.C., Chicago, Atlanta, Florida, Memphis, Texas, Los Angeles, San Francisco, and the Pacific Northwest.

In addition to presenting the annual television show, and a Latin version as well, the organization holds educational meetings and seminars in its various chapters. It can be a good source of networking with record labels, record producers, songwriters, and artists. Membership requires your involvement on six cuts of a recording as an artist, backup singer or player, record producer, songwriter, or recording engineer. Other categories include album cover artists or writers of liner notes. People who haven't fulfilled the eligibility requirements can also join as associate members. One of the benefits of membership is that the organization makes new CDs available at discount prices to members.

NARAS also has grant programs that involve various aspects of the record industry, scholarships for music students, and a presentation in high school educational events called Grammy in the Schools.

The Songwriters Guild

Another organization of interest to songwriters is the Songwriters Guild of America. They provide sample publishing contracts, somewhat weighted in favor of the songwriter, as opposed to the music publisher. They also will pursue legal action for the songwriter who is not being paid royalties for her work. They take a small percentage of whatever monies they are able to recover for the writer in exchange for this service.

By the way, should you be short of money and need services from a music business attorney, you should consult the Volunteer Lawyers for the Arts, at 1 E. 53rd Street, New York, New York 10222–4201, 212-319-ARTS, www.vlany.org. They have branch organizations in many parts of the country. Their lawyers provide low-cost legal services, based on a musician's income.

BOOKING YOUR OWN SMALL CONCERTS

If you have a developing fan base from local club dates that is enthusiastic about your original songs, you might consider booking your own small concert. You will need to find a reasonably priced venue, establish your ticket price, print tickets, and do all of your own publicity.

This requires a lot of ambition and organization, but can be lucrative financially and will help build your fan base. Make sure you have someone to solicit folks' e-mail addresses when they walk in the door so you can begin to create an e-mail mailing list, if you do not already have one.

For the first twenty or so years of my career, I kept a voluminous surface mailing list that I mailed to monthly. Some artists and agents still send out gig listing and reminders using surface mail, but this can be very costly considering the cost of postage today.

E-mail, on the other hand, is cheap and easy to send, though it doesn't have quite the same impact. Still, it is an effective way to keep fans of your songs updated on what you are doing and where you are playing, and it is essential to harvest whatever contact information you can from your supporters as you make albums and perform more frequently.

An example of how you can make a small concert work for you:

1. Rent a 100-seat club or hall for $200.
2. Print tickets and posters, at a cost of $50. Charge a $10 admission per person.
3. Send out all promotional material in a timely fashion (standard rule of promotion: at least two press releases, one a month before the event, the other arriving at the newspaper two weeks before the event or whenever the publication deadline is, accompanied by a black-and-white glossy photo).
4. Follow up with phone calls to your press releases; call and get whatever free publicity you can obtain (radio/TV interviews).
5. Take out an ad in an alternative paper in your community that your target audience tends to read—$100 or so.
6. You own your own PA system, so there is no PA cost. You play solo, so there are no side musicians to pay. Remember, the focus of the event is on you and your songs.
7. Invite any music business types to come to the concert on your guest list (music reviewers, independent record store owners, club owners of establishments where you want to perform).
8. Get every acquaintance and family member you know to attend the show. Give them complimentary tickets if you have to.

The big day comes. You sell 100 tickets, and give away 60. You gross $1000 from ticket sales. You sell twenty of your new CDs at $15 each for another $300 of revenue. You create a buzz about yourself and hopefully have enticed some people to get more interested in your songs and obtained at least 100 new names for your mailing list. You have cleared $650 after expenses, plus another $300 from CD sales.

As in all professions, sometimes it takes an investment of money and belief in yourself, along with self-promotion, to make money and to progress.

This is a good time to mention the skill of being able to write a coherent press release and to learn to perform the various tasks you need to do to promote yourself, in print and otherwise. It is a good investment as a songwriter/performer to take a class in public relations or journalism, to hone the practical writing skills you already have, and to learn about the marketing aspect of your career. There are short day and night classes available at community colleges on these topics that are very affordable. There are also seminars and workshops at many music festivals on how to do these tasks and what is expected of you as a promoter of your own music.

Later in your career, if you are fortunate, you may have an agent, manager, or publicist to perform some of these tasks for you. However, like every other facet of this career, you had better know how it all works, and be able to do it yourself.

Very Important!

Hold on to every newspaper article, every television story done about you—literally, any bit of publicity your music and you are able to garner. This is how promotional packages are constructed; this is the way careers are made. Be very careful with this material; you can never replace it when it is lost, particularly notices from early in your artistic life. File it all carefully and use it judiciously; it is more valuable than gold, and you cannot buy it.

House Concerts

An alternative to promoting your own small concert is to get a fan, family friend, or someone who regularly does them to put on a house concert for you.

House concerts are a variation on the time-honored tradition of people getting together at someone's home and sharing and listening to music they enjoy.

Today, most house concerts are events where a performer is invited to do two 45-minute acoustic sets for a small but appreciative audience. The host usually provides coffee and light snacks, and invites friends to attend. The performer generally coordinates with the host to help promote the show too. It is an intimate and respectful atmosphere, particularly for acoustic music.

Most house concerts range from ten to fifty people in attendance. Admission is generally $8 to $15, most or all of which goes to the performer at the end of the night.

Between the admission and CD sales, it can be a very lucrative night for the performer, and a wonderful way for the audience to connect with the artist in a very personal situation.

TURNING POINTS IN ARTISTS' CAREERS AND HOW THEY OCCURRED

Everyone has different needs and desires in life, so obviously there is no single standard of success in art. That is part of the beauty and joy of discovery, but also part of the frustration in deciding if you have the talent, stubbornness, work ethic, and organization to do it as your life's work.

However, if things are going to work out for you to do songwriting and performing as more than an avocation, you need a break somewhere along the way. This is why you have performed so many solo gigs, worn out the vehicles and your eyes driving all of those miles, and sacrificed the home life and weekends most people take for granted: to get the break that will make things a little easier for you.

About the most I can say is that if you do have that talent and put in the hard work, something will happen for you. In my opinion, it doesn't hurt to be doing the music for the right reasons as well—the motivation for all the work being the music itself, and the message you are conveying through those songs.

Harry Manx summed it up well, I think, when he spoke about the turning point in his career:

> It was in Japan I finally started to make a decent living. But I really hadn't seen any great degree of success until I returned to Canada in the year 2000, and then I really started to get into the music business and started to receive the kind of income that I could survive well on.
>
> At that time I finally found out some aspect of my music that made me unique. It wasn't about how good I was anymore, it was just the fact that I was different and that came about by learning the Mohan Veena, the Indian instrument I play, suddenly made me stand out of the crowd. I think that was really the turning point, and even now, though it is not a huge part of what I do in the show, I have their attention with that instrument and they listen to the other stuff, too.
>
> For the first four and a half years I studied the Mohan Veena, I had no idea how to mix it into the other music I was doing. I actually didn't have any idea to do that. I was thinking I was going to learn this instrument. I had already started going over to the ashram and playing with tabla players. I thought this was my special thing, playing this instrument; it wasn't about putting it out there to the people. I was kind of selfish.
>
> After some years in India, we would be sitting around late at night, when we would jam. I would play a few blues things on the Mohan Veena, and these guys would roll over and laugh, and say, "That's really funny." They would want to learn how to bend the notes, and stuff like that. Then I realized, "I hope I'm not being sacrilegious, but maybe I could actually blend a bit of this."
>
> When I came back to Canada, I had the same feeling about not using it. When I went to open mikes, I just took my regular guitar.

People were pretty impressed with the songs I had written and the way that I could play, but they didn't know that I played Indian music and the Mohan Veena. Then one show, I brought the Veena, and I saw the response was pretty strong. People were saying, "What is that?" That is when my eyes opened and I realized that this was the way I could get some attention for my music. I began to bring it out more, and to play some Western songs on it.

I never really set out to do that, and I was just as surprised as everyone that it had that effect on people.

In Chapter 2, Gordon Lightfoot talked about how important his signing with the Grossman organization was. Grossman/Court also began to place his songs with established artists, and soon after that dozens of singers in varied genres began including Lightfoot compositions on their records.

Another pivotal event for Lightfoot was when "Ribbon of Darkness" became a Top Ten charting country music hit in the 1960s.

I think that they got it off of my first album from someone down there in Nashville, and decided to speed it up by about a third. Marty Robbins did a wonderful job on the song, it was lovely, and I even got a chance to meet him at one point. They took the song and sped it up, which is how I would have done it if I had done it again.

Things were moving very rapidly at this time for Lightfoot. In a short period of time, he went from playing for $125 a week at Steele's Tavern on Yonge Street in Toronto to headlining sold-out shows at the Riverboat Coffeehouse on Yorkville Avenue, at the then-unheard-of pay scale of $1000 per week.

For the amount of work that was going to be done, it was a fair sum. I had to do a lot of shows, but that was good. That is what got me polished. Bernie Fiedler [owner of the Riverboat] became a friend and is still a friend. [40 years later, Fiedler is the promoter of Lightfoot's 2006 to 2007 cross-Canada concert tour.]

At the Riverboat, the press came in, which was very important. When you did the Riverboat, you were bound to get a review in the newspaper.

At the Riverboat they listened. But even at Steele's Tavern in Toronto, before the Riverboat days, they [the audiences] were surprisingly good. I enjoyed it all.

By the time the spring of 1990 rolled around, I had already been a full-time performing singer/songwriter for almost twenty years. In

1986 I had begun a folk music radio broadcast, *River City Folk,* on a local public radio station in Omaha, Nebraska. I was paid nothing for doing it the first year and a pittance after that. I did it because I believed in the music and thought it deserved to be heard in my community.

In 1990 a statewide public radio network was being established in Nebraska. Reading this in the newspaper, I arranged a meeting with the new manager of that network. His name was Steve Robinson, and he showed interest in *River City Folk* being heard as a two-hour show on the new statewide network. I told him what I thought was a fair rate of pay for me to produce the show in Omaha; he said he would think about it.

A few weeks later, there was a reception in Norfolk, Nebraska, for one of the new affiliates of that network. Steve Robinson suggested I might come to that on the off-chance of meeting his boss, who was very well connected with the state legislature at that time. So I made the 100-mile drive up there that April afternoon and got to meet the money manager of the network for all of about 30 seconds. I still did not have an answer about whether the show would go statewide, but a few days later I found out the decision was "yes."

In 1991 that station, KVNO at the University of Nebraska at Omaha, obtained the funding for my program to become a national broadcast on the National Public Radio satellite. Two years later, I was commissioned by the university to host thirty-two episodes of a television version of *River City Folk,* which was a joint venture between the university and the Americana Cable Network out of Branson, Missouri.

The television show was seen on Public Television across Nebraska, and all across the United States on the Americana Cable Network. It is still seen in reruns in Omaha today, eleven years later. The radio version of *River City Folk* is heard on over 150 NPR and other public radio affiliates each week, and is currently syndicated by the WFMT Radio Network out of Chicago. XM Satellite Radio also carries *River City Folk* three or four times a week on Channel 15, the Village.

All of this started from a little local radio broadcast in a medium-sized Midwestern city. It has opened more doors for me than I can count, and I have always been convinced it all happened because the love of the music was the genesis of it all.

Eliza Gilkyson is enjoying great success now, and each album seems to be more successful and receive more critical acclaim than the one before, but it certainly hasn't always been that way for her. It was a rocky road to success, just as it is for most folks in this profession.

I made some mistakes. I can look back and see three times I made decisions that I can't blame anyone else for, but at the time I was constantly seeking some kind of significant relationship, a partner, who would help me make my dream come true. My first husband was a lead guitar player, and he was supposed to be the person who would help me make it happen. My second husband was a manager, and I just turned myself over to his vision of who I should be, and I did the same thing with a third partner, where I just didn't take charge of my own career. I kept trying to find a mate who would do it for me. You can't blame them; they did the best they could. It was just me not taking responsibility for my life and not taking charge of my career.

The times that I did that, I just turned left on tangents that did not serve me well.

There was a point about six or seven years ago when I realized I was not going to be the next big anything, and that my dream of what I thought I was going to do with my life was over. That was the point I realized I was going to be a very bitter person who failed at what her life's dream was, or I was going to make another life beautiful for me. It was like once I realized that door to commercial success closed, I turned around and embraced what my life truly is. It is not the world of fame and fortune, it is a whole trajectory that is meaningful, rewarding, lucrative, and satisfying for me—but I didn't know that until I had to go through this grieving period that I had to let go of what I thought my life was supposed to be. When I did that, that was when I decided I was going to go out on the road... . I was almost fifty. I was going to go out in the van, I'm going to say yes to every gig, I'm going to take $50 for shows in new markets, I'm just going to do whatever it takes. At my age, it felt humiliating to go through that process, because I felt like I had a lot of talent and gifts that I had acquired over the years, and I had to start completely over, with nothing, basically.

That was the best thing that ever happened to me. I just gave myself to the muses in a way I never had before. Before I had always been posturing myself, and trying to be this, trying to play that game. I had a manager who tried to help me shape myself into something that would be commercially viable. When I let go of that, when I realized I was too old, it was like "Yay!" ... and that was the best thing that ever happened to me.

ARTS COUNCIL CONCERTS, COMMUNITY CONCERT SERIES, AND OTHER CULTURAL PRESENTERS

A further substantial source of income for the performing singer/songwriter can be performances for arts councils and other cultural organizations.

Most states have touring arts programs, even after recent reductions in federal funding for the arts. These are often difficult programs to get into, but can be very lucrative. They also greatly value original material or art/music that is somehow educational, historical, or outside mainstream culture.

You will generally have to establish a price and put together a sample touring budget for these programs, as well as explain in depth why your performance has the kind of merit that should be included in the touring roster. You will also have to show what kind of promotional materials you will use, and provide a sample contract.

After you are accepted into the program, you will be included in their directory. Either you or your agent still has to solicit your own concerts and establish the date, though the price is set. You provide the arts organization that hires you for the concert the promotional materials, and it is their job to get people to come to the show.

You receive your established price for the concert, no matter how many people come. This price is usually anywhere from $600 to $5000.

Each U.S. state and Canadian province has its own arts council or commission you can consult with to see how touring works in your region and if support for it is available where you live.

I toured for fourteen years with the Nebraska Arts Council touring program and was later accepted into the Mid-America Arts Alliance touring program as well. Both were good experiences for me. Doing arts council concerts added approximately $12,000 to $15,000 income to me each of those years, and I had many wonderful audiences.

There are also young audience concert programs funded by cities, states, school systems, and arts councils, which can be an important monetary supplement to a performing singer/songwriter's career. These are performances in schools, but keep in mind that developing programs for children of various ages requires some thought and experimentation.

Another opportunity to reach many people is the community concert. These are primarily booked by private agencies. The advantage of agency-booked community concert series gigs is that they do the booking for you. The disadvantage is that they generally take half of the fee as commission.

The selection process is rigorous, and if you are accepted in the program you will need to be very flexible in your travel schedule. Most community concerts are sold to the audiences as multiperformance packages, so you never know what kind of an audience you will get, either in size or enthusiasm. Still, these concerts are a wonderful way for a performer to truly make a living doing music, if you are able to make the adjustments in your life to adapt to the travel schedule.

Community concert series generally pay in the $1000 to $3000 range for a solo artist, and much more than that for ensembles. You are generally liable for your own travel expenses out of that amount.

Many museums and libraries also offer concerts to the general public and to their members. Most of these sorts of performances are booked by the individual museum or handled by an agent who is working to book the series for them. These can be lucrative shows, and it is worth investigating opportunities with local institutions of these kinds in your area. Often they have educational grants or other monies specifically earmarked for musical offerings.

Many larger communities also have "Music in the Parks" programs. Some of these are sponsored by a fund administered by the Musicians' Union and you have to belong to the union to perform, but many other parks' concert series are independently funded and can be both a profitable and audience-building gig.

You can usually find out more about these opportunities by contacting the Parks and Recreation Department in your town or by inquiring at City Hall.

RECORDING YOUR FIRST ALBUM

After you have done your first demo and experimented with the recording process, which is very different than playing your songs at home or in a public performance setting, it's time to start planning your first album.

When you decide to record your own album, there are a number of issues involved. Here are some of the most important of these considerations:

- What is the budget for the project?
- Are you paying for the project yourself or are you borrowing money from your family or friends? Are there people investing in the project?
- Once the recording is completed, do you have a plan to promote it? Do you have distribution or do you plan to consign the album in stores?
- Do you have digital distribution?

- Will you get any radio play for the project?

In my experience, some of the most creative projects fail because the artist has not considered where the album will be sold.

Below are some of the advantages and disadvantages of "doing it yourself."

On the plus side:

- You control the budget.
- You control the entire creative process, including such details as the album cover and notes.
- No one can pressure you to finish the album before you are satisfied with it.
- You get all or most of the income from sales of the album.

On the minus side:

- Unless you are independently wealthy, there are probably severe limitations on how much money you will be able to spend.
- You will need to budget quite a bit of time to the business of promoting and selling the record—time that will take away from your ability to create and practice your music.
- Unless you are extremely disciplined, you are very likely to waste time and money in the studio.

Recording, and the recording process, is where the experience of being a performing singer/songwriter has most radically changed since the time when I began my career. Since 1972, the year I began my career, until now, the number of album releases has grown from 7,000 per year to over 45,000 per year.

I did my first demo in a closet in Toronto on a stereo Revox quarter-inch tape machine. A couple of years later, I had the opportunity to work after hours with an intern at Universal Recording Studios in Chicago on some very advanced equipment for that time (1974). I completed my first demo there with the help of an intern who was encouraged to practice in the off-hours at the studio.

When I finally recorded my first album in 1978, it was done at a 16-track studio outside of Toronto (The Grange, in Whitby, Ontario—long since closed). The studio rate was about $50 per hour, plus the four $180 rolls of 2-inch tape.

I used about 50 hours recording that album. With inflation, that would equate to right around $12,000 in costs today.

Though he had recorded a couple of singles and a live club album with his early duo partner Terry Whelan, Gordon Lightfoot began his recording career in earnest in 1965 when he went to New York to put down his first album, *Lightfoot,* for United Artists records.

> For the first album, I don't think they had more than 8 tracks in 1965. Later on, they had 16. That stuff was all done live off of the floor anyway. All of my albums are still done live, off of the floor (guitar and vocals together), except for the last album [*Harmony*], which got done in the hospital.

Incidentally, Lightfoot says he's back to 99 percent, after a long illness.

Gordon Lightfoot's first albums were on United Artists. Previous to that, a small Canadian company released a couple of singles early in his career.

A very few artists then released their own albums in those days. To press 1000 of them cost around $2500 in the 1970s, after the recording, artwork, and other preparation was done. If you sold them from the stage, the going rate was $7 per record.

Making an album, then and now, is like buying a car: you can spend whatever you can afford. The saying around the music industry today is "Any musician with a credit card can make a CD," and it is probably true.

Today, you should be able to record in a good digitally equipped studio, with decent microphones, for around $35 per hour. This price will include an engineer (generally the owner) who will work with you. This price is for a fairly basic studio, but if you know what you want you can still get a good product.

If you want a producer to assist you, you will need to hire him and pay for him yourself. We will talk more about the role of producers in the recording process in a later chapter. The help of a producer on an album is helpful at any time in your recording experience, but most songwriters cannot afford an experienced producer until later in their career.

I recently recorded an album that I wanted a "live" kind of sound for, to sell from the stage at a Celtic music gig I do. I recorded it at Medicine Whistle Studios, a small, but very well-equipped studio in Portland. My band and I did not take a long time putting down the tracks, but I was amazed at the quality that is now available for a more-than-reasonable price. I produced it myself, and recorded it for less than $1500.

I have had thirty-five years of studio experience, so I knew what I was doing and what I wanted. However, thirty years ago the same project would have cost me four times as much, or more!

There are many studios that will be more expensive than that $35 per hour figure, and depending on your goals for the sound of the album, the extra price can be well worth it. Eliza Gilkyson talks about her early recording experience, and why she still values the analog sound, which adds cost to the process:

The first album I made was called *Eliza*, in 1969. That was my first album, but I had been recording with my dad for years at that point. I would do a song for him in Hollywood, or wherever, recording his demos, and then he would let me have an hour at the end of his time to do my thing.

The first studio I sang in was Goldstar Studios on Sunset Blvd. It was a 16-track, 2-inch-tape, analog studio.

There is a picture on my Web site, in the biography section, of me singing with my dad when I was about 5. He was using a big old Neumann microphone in that picture.

I have been using a Manley microphone in the studio for my most recent albums.

On *Hard Times in Babylon*, I went on to tape and dumped onto Pro Tools for overdubs, mixing, and editing, and I did the same thing with *Lost and Found*.

For *Land of Milk and Honey*, we recorded onto digital and ran it through tape, because it is so much easier to record onto digital.

On the most recent album, *Paradise Hotel*, we ran the digital tracks through a tape program. The tape program just now bumped up to an acceptable level for me to give that recording a nice analog sound, after the digital recording, so that is what we did.

I tell performers if they are really planning on doing a record right, paying their musicians and producer fairly, and taking all the time you need, that it takes about $20,000.

That monetary figure can be argued, both as being too low and as being too high, but I totally agree with Gilkyson that the analog process adds warmth and dimension to recordings, particularly for acoustic instruments and music where the quality of the vocal is paramount. I recorded an album in 2001 at Big Red Recording Studios in the foothills of Mt. Hood, Oregon. The equipment there includes vintage Neumann microphones and a mixing board that came out of the "Automat" recording studio in San Francisco. That board was an integral part of the sound Aretha Franklin and Stevie Wonder achieved on some of their biggest selling albums, and owner/engineer Billy Oskay uses it brilliantly. He charges by the day rather than the hour, and totally immerses himself in the project. He and I, together with my producer Clete Baker, put together an album, *Vested*, that is still the favorite of all of my records.

That recording was also the most expensive I have done to date, but I believe it was money well spent.

Nonetheless, spending a lot of money on an album project certainly does not guarantee a superior result. The songs themselves and the way they are sung and arranged are far more important in the end. Spending only a little money, however, does not necessarily doom a project to mediocrity, if the material is fresh and the artist knows how to make the studio process work within his or her budget.

If you are working as a solo singer/songwriter, you should be able to put together a 10-song basic album with minimal accompaniment (bass, lead guitar, and/or piano) for between $1000 and $2000 at that rate of $35 an hour. This includes recording time, some overdubs, and mix-down time.

Of course, this is totally dependent on how picky you are, how accomplished a musician you have become, and how comfortable you are working in the studio. The studio is a totally different environment than any other live performance situation.

If you need drums or percussion, add on half again as much total time as you are planning on. Miking, recording, and mixing drums and percussion requires much more time at each stage of the process.

The key to getting a project like this done quickly and efficiently is having the songs rehearsed well and the arrangements you are going to use well thought out, making sure the other musicians are scheduled for when you need them there, and having any overdubs you are going to use well rehearsed.

In my experience, and the experience of other musicians' producers I have talked to over the years, overdubs will generally take twice as long as you have planned to get them right. Plan accordingly, and try not to be too ambitious with your overdub use if you want to stay within your budget.

You may want to master your project when it is done, to smooth out the rough edges and make it sound more polished. Add on another $400 to $800 for that step.

Mastering is like polishing a piece of jewelry: even though the mixes may be good, the mastering will make the total sound shine by making sure all the sound frequencies and the stereo imaging of the instruments work well. If there is great volume disparity between tracks, the mastering engineer will (hopefully) slightly compress the sound of the louder tracks to give the album a cohesive feel.

Not every album absolutely needs to be mastered, but it is a step that will improve any album.

If you are on a tight budget, you can often master your album in the studio where you recorded it at a much lower hourly rate than a mastering studio will charge.

Just as if you have a budget from a record company, establish a budget that you can live with for recording the album; set up a schedule of benchmarks you want to achieve (such as how many overdubs you want to complete in a day), and attempt to stick to it; and place a limit on how long you will spend on mix-down. (There are *always* more things that can be changed in mix-down; at some point, you just have to let it be.)

After you complete the recording process, it will cost you around $1100 to $1500 to get the discs pressed, inserts put in, and the CD packaged, to get 1000 copies of your CD into your hands. Add the cost of your artwork, photos, and cover design to this cost. Again, this figure changes depending on the packaging you choose and the quantity of your order.

In 1991, I produced a first album for a very talented Wyoming-based songwriter by the name of Chris Kennedy. We were pleased by the way the arrangements and the recordings came out.

The title track of the album, *Away from It All,* was a song about a couple escaping from urban bustle to the joys of rural Wyoming life. In the song, he mentioned a roadhouse in Farson called the Oregon Trail Café.

Passing through Farson, excited about the results of the project, Chris stopped into the café with a copy of the album and told the owner (who was flipping burgers at the time) about the song and about the mention of the café. Chris handed him a cassette that he anticipated the owner might enjoy or might even play in the café for his customers.

The owner of the Oregon Trail Café took a long look at the cassette, and said, "We don't listen to music much around these parts."

So be aware that the response to your early efforts may not always be what you hope for, though completing that first album is absolutely key to a songwriter/performer's career.

THE ROLE OF RADIO AND OTHER MEDIA: HOW TO GET YOUR SONGS PLAYED

Once your album is completed and you want to get your songs heard by a wider audience on radio:

- Identify stations in your own area that play a format similar to the songs you are writing yourself. Call or otherwise make contact and ask if they are open to listening to, and possibly playing, one of your songs on the air. (Bear in mind that public radio stations are generally the most open to receiving new CDs; formatted pop radio stations, except for whatever specialty programs they may feature, are more closed to new music.)

- Using an Internet search engine such as Google, find twenty radio stations playing the kind of music that is featured on your CD (country, pop, Americana, folk, etc.). Collect those stations' addresses and phone numbers.
- Make phone contact with each station, first finding out if they are open to new material from unsigned writers. If they are, find out who to send the material to at the station.
- Send out the material, and follow up with a call two to three weeks after you do, to see if they have aired your music. Ask your contact at the station if he or she has any suggestions for you for other airplay possibilities.

Radio remains an important element to building a career as a singer/songwriter.

The radio industry continues to change at a rapid pace as more and more independent radio stations are gobbled up by huge media companies. On commercial radio, the latitude that individual disc jockeys or stations once had to break a new record to its audience has virtually disappeared. That kind of personal radio has been replaced with "formats" constructed in New York, L.A., or Nashville and sold to the conglomerate stations.

In 1970, Gordon Lightfoot's song "If You Could Read My Mind" became his first U.S. hit, after a string of successes in Canada. It would not have happened, however, without the initiative of a Seattle disc jockey who fell in love with that song when it was released on the album *Sit Down Young Stranger,* on Warner/Reprise. The DJ played it for his listeners repeatedly as an album cut, and it received tremendous response. Hearing of this Pacific Northwest development, the Reprise Records folks reprinted the album with the new title *If You Could Read My Mind* and released a new 45-rpm single with that name. It rose to the American Top Ten and gave Lightfoot the boost he had needed to become a major U.S. songwriting/performing/recording success. He was able to follow up that song with "Sundown," "The Wreck of the Edmund Fitzgerald," and other singles that remain popular today, and established himself as a concert draw around the world.

Unfortunately, today such a scenario as what happened with Lightfoot's breakthrough song "If You Could Read My Mind" would be impossible. Neither the radio nor the record industry works that way anymore.

There are still, however, many opportunities for songwriters to have their albums and songs heard on the airwaves.

"Public Radio" is a blanket term for a number of different kinds of FCC licenses, including university stations, community radio stations, and student-run stations. All of these have some kind of mix of music independent from the commercial radio formulas.

It is a general misconception that National Public Radio is a blanket organization. Rather, it is a syndicating company; it offers programs or packages of programs to member and associate member stations.

Other syndicating organizations include Public Radio International, the BBC, and the WFMT Radio Network (which distributes my program, *River City Folk*).

All Things Considered is an NPR show, but it is not heard on all public radio stations; even some stations that carry other NPR programming might not carry it.

I point this out to illustrate that if you want your songs played on public radio, you have to approach every station or every program individually.

As popular as *A Prairie Home Companion* might be on public radio, it is not heard everywhere in the United States. If you perform on *A Prairie Home Companion,* you will be heard on more than 400 stations across the United States. However, to be heard consistently on those and other stations, you will have to individually send a CD to each station that you want to have consider your music for airplay.

This is something a record label does if you have a contract with them—but even then, most successful artists follow up on the releases that are sent out, or have a publicist do it for them.

For artists trying to get played on radio for the first time, I suggest targeting a dozen radio stations that have programming that your recording would fit into. These are generally public radio stations or adult acoustic alternative (AAA) stations. Focus on stations that cover regions where you will be doing a gig, where you have performed before, or where you may have some kind of personal connection.

Send out your CD with a one-page description of the kind of music you play; what you have accomplished so far in your career; what your local connections are to that station, if any (such as song themes, family background, performance history, etc.); any positive reviews you have garnered for that CD or any other CDs you may have out; and any quotes you can obtain from other music industry people (club owners, festival directors, etc.).

Many artists and record labels also enclose a stamped, self-addressed card with some questions for the radio station to answer, such has how many times the record was played and what the listener response was. (They also solicit quotes for their promotional packages on these cards.) I personally do not think this step is worth the time and money it takes, but other artists and labels would disagree with me, arguing that the information they receive and the fan base they build offset the energy expenditure and the cost.

Within a respectable period of time after the release and accompanying material has been sent, many artists or publicists follow up by e-mail or phone and inquire as to whether the album was received and if it received airplay.

Altogether, it is a time-consuming and expensive process. There are extensive station promotional lists available from search engines on the Internet. You can also consult some of the stations we have listed in the bibliography of this book. However, if you are just beginning the process of distributing your CD to stations, I highly suggest you do some research and initially send them to just a few likely candidates in areas where you will be performing.

After all of that work, there is nothing quite like the thrill of first hearing your own song on the radio, either sung by yourself or someone else. Eliza Gilkyson talks about the first song of hers she heard being played over the airwaves:

> It was a song called "Rainmaker," when I was living in Santa Fe, from an early LP of this band I was in. It was a song about the drought, and dancing for rain. The day they released the song, the drought broke!

Gordon Lightfoot had a Canadian hit very early on in his career with a song that was recorded in Nashville, called "Remember Me, I'm the One." It was played on a major Toronto AM station, and all across Canada, in the very early 1960s.

He released it as part of his year 2000 boxed-set retrospective, *Songbook*, almost forty years after it had been released as a standalone single. That song predated his United Artist and Warner/Reprise albums, and gave him confidence in his songwriting ability.

Harry Manx was a full-time performer for many years, in many parts of the world, before he started to release albums. He was still excited and surprised to hear a song of his being played from his first album, even before it was officially released:

> I was driving through Alberta and heard one of my songs on CKUA. I had just recorded the *Dog, My Cat* album late in 2000 and I met Holgar Peterson from CKUA radio, who was on a fishing trip to Saltspring Island, where I live. We were at a party, and

he didn't know who I was, and I didn't know who he was. I played a song at the party, and he said, "Wow, that was good. Do you have a record?" I had just had a master made at the studio, and I pulled it out of my pocket and told him he could have that, if he wanted it. So he took it, and CKUA started playing that master, with no cover or anything. So I was driving through Alberta on my first little tour. I think I had six shows all across the country, all well attended by six people at each show. I heard my song on the radio, and I was thrilled. The first time is always the best. It was a Muddy Waters cover I recorded, "Can't Be Satisfied." He loved that version of the song and played it often on his blues show.

I mentioned both *A Prairie Home Companion* and my program *River City Folk* as syndicated shows that feature a wide range of singer/songwriters. Garrison Keillor once talked about how musicians tend to overplay the importance of appearing on his show. Overall, I would agree with him; a radio spot like performing two songs on *A Prairie Home Companion* cannot alone make your career. Rather, it is the accumulation of hundreds of gigs large and small that will turn the corner for you.

However, any time you have a chance to reach the potential audience that radio can offer you, it is important to take advantage of the chance. Most radio live appearances will be gratis, although some will pay a fair amount of money; all of them are important to building a career as a performer/songwriter.

After appearing on a local community radio broadcast, that station is also much more likely to play songs from your albums on their programming. Most of the people I book for the festivals that I direct I heard play live, a few feet from me, recording my *River City Folk* broadcast. There are many professional benefits to playing on the radio whenever you can that may not be immediately apparent, just as is true for the world of stage performances.

Listen to your local public stations and decide which programs might be approached about you doing some of your songs live on air. Most programs are independently produced, so you will have to contact the host of the show directly, rather than the station, to inquire about appearing on his or her show.

Dave Carter and Tracy Grammer, whom I also talk about in an upcoming chapter on festivals, helped launch a very successful career by pursuing and being willing to play on virtually any station that would let them perform.

Aside from *A Prairie Home Companion* and *River City Folk*, there are other broadcasts heard nationally that feature singer/songwriters performing live, including *Mountain Stage* from West Virginia; *E-Town* from Boulder, Colorado; *Folkstage* produced by Rick Warren for the WFMT Radio Network; and Nick Spitzer's *American Routes* in New Orleans. The competition to appear on these shows is stiff, but performing on shows such as these will be helpful footnotes to your bio, and your songs will be heard by many thousands of people.

4

TODAY'S ALBUM, CD, AND RECORD BUSINESS

Up until about ten years ago, making a record involved renting a recording studio in order to make a "demo" (demonstration record), and then finding some way to access a record label.

Today the variables are more complex. As mentioned in the previous chapter, artists record in their own home studios or in relatively small rooms rented out at relatively reasonable prices. They then make a determination of whether to rent out a more expensive studio in order to mix the product down or to complete the process in a home studio.

Certainly, a recording artist today is going to be competing in a much more crowded and competitive world of musical releases than when my first album was recorded and released in 1978.

Terry Currier (see Figure 4.1) has had a lifetime of owning and managing Music Millennium, one of the most successful independent record stores in the United States. In addition to keeping Music Millennium in the red, he also has a record label, Burnside Records, which specializes in blues artists, and a national/international record distribution company, BDC (Burnside Distribution), which handles dozens of independent labels.

Currier did an extensive interview regarding those varied facets of the record business. Speaking of one of the major differences in album marketing since he began his career in the 1970s, Currier says,

> In 1972, the year that I started in record retail, there were less than 7000 releases nationally. Last year there were 45,000 national releases in the United States.
>
> Recording became a lot more accessible to everyone. It used to be that you had to get the record deal to make it worthwhile to make the record.

Figure 4.1 Terry Currier. Courtesy of Terry Currier.

In the 1960s, when Mitch Miller was the head of A & R (artists and repertoire) for Columbia Records, he made the artists use Columbia's studio, and he was charging them $500 per hour for studio time. (Imagine that! It would be like charging around $2500 per hour today!)

Records were a lot cheaper at that time [around $3 to $4] but with that kind of methodology it would take a *long* time for the artist to recoup the money from the recording costs.

If the artist was in the studio for two weeks, that gave him a studio bill to pay off from the record royalties of right around $50,000 [more than $250,000 today!], excluding sideman musician fees, equipment rental, etc.

MAJOR LABELS: WHAT THEY DO AND HOW TO ACCESS THEM

At the present writing, there are four major labels: BMG-Sony, EMI (known as Capitol in the United States), Universal, and Warner Records. I use the term "at this writing," because EMI and Warner Records have been in discussions to unite for several years, BMG may well be sold, and Universal might be spun off from its French parent, Vivendi.

Artists who are seeking to attain mass popularity and worldwide distribution still gravitate to the major labels. Major labels enjoy international distribution and, should they decide to do so, are capable of investing large amounts of money in an artist. That money can be used to promote an artist through record store listening stations, print advertising, radio or television ads, the giving away of thousands of free CDs for review purposes, and even hiring additional independent promoters who are not on staff with the record company. They may also provide tour support in the early part of an artist's career, so that the artist can go out on a financially unprofitable tour that will produce valuable exposure for that artist. Usually major label deals are accessed either through a personal manager or an entertainment business lawyer. Generally they do not accept unsolicited tapes, and they usually prefer not to have any business dealings with an artist.

This is not to say that all personal managers or entertainment lawyers have an open door at major labels, because they too are screened out to avoid the amateur or ill-prepared entrepreneur. One of the true tests of a manager or entertainment lawyer is her willingness to believe in an act enough to accept the inevitable rejection notices that some companies will give her, and to keep on promoting the act. Remember that the Beatles were turned down by every record company in England—twice! If you read biographies of other top recording acts, almost all of them suffered frequent rejection before finally landing a major-label deal. If two or three rejections cause your representative to cease believing in your talent, then you probably need to consider finding other people to represent you.

Wild Cards

Once in a very great while, a record company A&R (artist and repertoire) representative wanders into a performance by accident, or because he had come to see an act, and he falls in love with an act that he didn't come to see. This can result in a record deal for that artist. Similarly, sometimes an unsolicited CD gets through the elaborate screening mechanisms that major labels construct to filter them out, and a record company executive finds a previously unknown group and signs them. It is also true that someone has to win the Powerball lottery. Unfortunately, the chances are that neither the unknown singer/songwriter nor the lottery ticket buyer is going to emerge victorious.

MONEY AND MAJOR RECORD LABELS

A major-label deal can result in a large advance payment to the artist. The artist needs to be aware that this advance, along with all of the expenses of making a CD, including the producer's fee and anywhere from 50 to 100 percent of the costs of making a video, are charged against the artist's royalties. Additional charges are made for the hiring of independent promotion people, lower royalties are paid for record club sales and foreign sales, and no money is paid to the artist when records are given away to radio stations or media critics. This whole process has been thoroughly documented in numerous books about the music business, and we recommend some of these in the bibliography at the end of this book. The bottom line is that because of all of these charge-backs, few recording artists actually make much money from the sales of their recordings.

Drummer Jacob Schlicter was in the band Semisonic. In his book *So You Want to Be a Rock and Roll Star,* he documents how the band never received any royalties despite having a million-selling record. The problem was that their previous recordings had lost money, and the band had made several videos. All of these charge-backs enabled the record company, MCA (now part of Universal Records), to legally avoid the necessity of paying the band any royalties.

There is a general feeling among people who have been active in the record industry for some years that the willingness of major labels to take a chance on developing new artists has become smaller, as the industry has been challenged by bootleg records and unauthorized digital downloads. All of the major labels except for BMG are on the stock market, and the bottom line is inevitably of great concern to the shareholders and to the people running the labels. The reality of dealing with major labels today is that if an act doesn't quickly show signs of achieving significant success, the label will probably drop the artist. This was somewhat less true during the era 1960 to 1980, when, for example, John Denver was carefully nurtured by RCA Victor through several unsuccessful albums before he hit pay dirt for the company.

ROYALTIES

Although royalties in major-label contracts indicate that the artist will receive a royalty of 10 to 12 percent of the retail selling price of a CD, and superstars can get as high as 20 percent, the various deductions in these contracts make these rates misleading. The more famous a producer that the artist chooses to use, the higher that producer's royalty rate and advance will be, and that will be deducted from the artist's royalties. The bottom line is, don't expect to make money on the sales of your records. By the way, even if you are fortunate enough to have a successful record, the following things may occur:

- If you are in debt to the record company from making earlier records that were not successful, that debt will be charged against your new royalties.
- Unfortunately, you won't be paid for months after the initial sales of the CD. The record company will usually hold 20 to 25 percent of the money in reserves, in case stores return some of your records that they ordered.

INDEPENDENT LABELS

Obviously from the numbers of album releases today, not everyone has to, or wants to, record for a major label. There are numerous independent labels, often specializing in a particular musical niche, such as blues or alternative rock music. These labels will not spend nearly as much money on producing or marketing your CD, but they may have a much better grasp of the particular musical style that you favor and where the market is for that musical genre. Because they generally put out fewer records and necessarily have tighter budgets, these independent labels may have better contact with your potential audience. I once heard an independent label owner rant that he had attended a music business conference where a music label executive had publicly stated that he loved the small independent labels, because they took the musical and financial risks and then the major labels could simply move in with a great deal of money and buy out an artist's contract, or find another artist to compete in that genre.

Terry Currier of Music Millennium spoke about how he decides what percentage of major labels and independent labels he carries in his stores:

> The national average is between 20 to 23 percent independents, and the rest major labels. In our case, we're over 50 percent independent in what we carry. We have large blues, world music, classical, and folk sections that you just won't find in other stores.
>
> If Josh Grobin is on Oprah, sales for his album will be big the next day at the mall stores and big box retailers. Things like that really don't affect my store, but there are things that do. An independent artist that can get a good story in a reputable publication, online or offline, with music credibility, can help them/us sell records.
>
> It used to be, in the seventies if you had a review in *Rolling Stone* magazine, that was a creditable magazine and it would sell lots of records. Today, they don't have the same credibility, because they are more of a lifestyle magazine. However, if you get a review in *MOJO* magazine, out of the United Kingdom, which has good distribution in the United States, and they start talking about someone in there, that can really help a blues record a lot.

Independent labels are generally much more accessible to artists, and a careful reading of the industry magazine *The Music Connection* reveals that a surprising number of them accept unsolicited demos. They also are more committed to music experimentation, because they understand that in many ways their best buy for success is to jump onto a new musical style before the major labels are even aware that the style exists.

Wearing his artist and repertoire hat for Burnside Records, Terry Currier talked about the principal reasons he decides to sign artists to his label:

> From an independent-label perspective, way different from the major-label perspective, the independent-label people are signing people because of the passion of the music. In my case, with Burnside Records, we felt that the music was strong enough that we could take it to a certain sales level. Our philosophy was, we could take it to that breakeven point and beyond. We could help artists with their careers by getting their music out there. But the main key for every record I have ever done is that it was something that I—100 percent—believed in the music. We never did a project, ever, just because we thought it had sales potential. We had to believe in the music.

It's not a totally rational business decision, and that's why lots of independent labels come and go.

I've seen people manage bands, and eventually become full-time managers, just because they liked someone's music. It's the music that hits the nerve. It's a good philosophy, because if you really believe in the music you'll put that 110 percent into the project.

The major labels use that philosophy less than they ever have, today. You look at the early seventies and the industry really took a big swing. A lot of people that went to work for the major labels came out of retail stores. It was a lot of independent stores like the Music Millenniums of the world that a lot of today's record executives and the record execs of the eighties and nineties came out of.

The positive side of working with an independent label is that there will probably be much more direct communication with the label, and often there is more sympathy with less conventional artists' musical objectives or even album covers. The negative side is that often artists' royalties are lower because the label doesn't control its own distribution, and in general smaller labels simply don't have the kind of promotional muscle that major labels have at their command.

Many fans and musicians believe that independent labels are intrinsically more honest than the majors are. If you accept this generalization, you may very well live to regret it. Unfortunately, you must exercise the same degree of care in dealing with small labels that you would in dealing with the giants. There are both honest and questionable people operating large and small labels.

If you are working in an extremely avant-garde or obscure musical genre, the choice is generally made for you: the major labels simply won't see your music as being commercially viable.

ARTIST-OWNED LABELS

Over the years, various artists have produced and marketed their own records. With the advent of home recording and relatively inexpensive CD duplication, this has become a much more practical option. I will return to this option shortly, but before we get into a bit more detail on that subject, there are also a number of artist-owned labels that have become quite successful. The group Mannheim Steamroller, headquartered in Omaha, has had a number of million-selling albums. Singer/songwriter Ani DiFranco owns a label called Righteous Babe, in her hometown of Buffalo, New York. Conor Oberst (Bright Eyes) is a part owner of the fiercely independent and successful Saddle Creek Records, also operating in Omaha. Righteous Babe and Saddle Creek release records by other artists as well as their owners, although in both cases, the labels' most successful artists are DiFranco and Oberst.

If you plan to produce and sell your own records, there are a few realities that you need to consider. As mentioned more than once in this book, you will probably sell the bulk of your CDs at your live performances. If you do not perform live with some regularity, then the chances are that you aren't going to sell many records. You should also be reconciled to the notion that because you are a relatively unknown artist on a completely unknown record label, the chances are that you will get little or no radio play.

It is quite possible to sell your albums on consignment at local record stores, but you will then need to carefully inventory all of your consignment items, and you will need to call on the stores to collect what they owe you. Don't expect that they will pay you without prompting.

Terry Currier of Music Millennium gives some suggestions to independent artists trying to place their music in stores:

> Go into a store like Music Millennium and establish a personal relationship with those record stores. You can personally deliver your records and work with that particular store to make things happen.
>
> For an independent artist-owned label that is, say, based in New York, trying to cover the whole United States—the first thing they can do is get the music out to the right stores, so they can hear it. They are going to have to make follow-up calls to get people to listen to it. Me, as buyer, today, for an independent record store—you can imagine the amount of promotional copies we get in the door, and don't have time to listen to. I try to listen to as many things as I possibly can, but I can't get through it all.
>
> So you have to be kind of semi-aggressive to have your head bob above the water of the sea of releases that are out there.

A final option is to try to deal with an independent record distributor to place your album into other markets. If you only have one album out, it will probably be difficult for you to find an independent distributor, and the chances are that they will be rather slow in paying you for whatever product that they sell.

If you decide to make and sell your own recording, get hold of the book *How to Make and Sell Your Own Record* by Diane Sward Rapaport (5th edition).

RECORD CONTRACTS AND MUSIC
PUBLISHING ROYALTIES

If at all possible, it is advantageous for the singer/songwriter not to give up publishing rights to his or her record label. Remember that the publishing income from the sales of a CD is 9.1 cents a song, usually split 50–50 between the songwriter and the publisher. If you are able to retain your publishing rights, you will keep all of that 9.1 cents. Another alternative is that you can give up the publishing rights to a publishing company for a large advance against royalties. Your record company will almost certainly resist this notion, because they will say that they are already making a heavy investment in your career. An outside music publishing company cannot very well make this argument.

Another fly in the ointment is that if the record company owns your music publishing rights, they may then charge the money from songwriting that you earn through them against your debt to the record company.

Independent labels, by the way, are much more apt to attempt to grab your publishing rights than the major companies are. For the artist in general, the most advantageous situation occurs when an artist is being sought after by more than one record company. Under these circumstances it is obvious that even a rookie manager will not allow the artist to give up his or her publishing rights to the record company.

Remember that music publishing income includes not only money derived from record sales but also income derived from the use of a song in a film or television show, print music rights, and so on.

RECORD DISTRIBUTION

The major record labels all control their own distribution. They have branches all over the United States and Canada in addition to their own labels, and they often distribute independent labels as well. There are also a handful of national independent distributors who distribute product in a similar manner but do not own the product that they distribute. In some markets there are also regional or statewide distributors who distribute records in a smaller territory. The biggest advantage of working with a major-label distribution company is that they are certainly going to remain in business and will pay their bills. The worst aspect of working with them is that your product is only the faintest blip on their radar screen, and they are not going to exert much effort to get your record into retail stores.

Terry Currier of Music Millennium gives us a brief timeline to help us understand the development of record distribution since the 1970s:

The first real record distribution company didn't really happen until 1972, and that was WEA. It was really the forging of those three labels [Warner, Elektra, Atlantic].

In the seventies they were really quite creative. It was more music driven than money driven. They had the philosophy that they didn't have to make their nut on the first record, or even the second record. They could work with an artist over a multi-record or multiyear deal to try and develop them.

Towards the end of the seventies and into the eighties, money interests started getting more involved because music was perceived as a sexy thing. Especially when the CD took off, a lot of money people really gravitated towards buying major record distributors. At one time, Seagram's owned Universal Music Group.

A lot of these majors are now owned by companies based in other countries. In the seventies, most of the major labels were owned by people who came out of the music base of the industry. Once money people started getting into the equation, it changed it a lot.

Historically, independent distributors have been slow in paying labels. This is because they in turn need to be paid by record stores, and also because, particularly in the case of small labels, the distributor may feel that since the label has no other product that the distributor wants, why should they hasten to pay the money due to them? The larger the distributor is, the less likely an independent artist is to be able to convince the distributor to carry his or her CD. If the artist is, for example, from Des Moines, and only plays in the immediate vicinity, why would the distributor want to place the album in stores in Albuquerque? The larger independent distributors also have literally dozens and dozens of labels, and it is just as easy for you to get lost in the shuffle as it is with a major label distributor. Of course, it is a bit of a moot point, because it is extremely unlikely that the major-label distributor will take on your CD.

One Stops, Rack Jobbers, and Mail-Order Catalogs

A one stop is a distributor that carries product from virtually all labels. They even carry major-label product at a slight markup. For a mom-and-pop record dealer in small-town America, dealing with a one stop is attractive because they can order everything from a single source and save on delivery costs, phone calls, and time.

Rack jobbers actually either own space in a large discount store or simply service the record department. Rack jobbers stock the records and will essentially run a record department for a department or discount store. They also service military bases' stores, which can sell quite a few albums.

Mail-order catalogs work like the old Sears catalogs. They develop a mailing list of people interested in music and send out mailings, usually offering some level of discounting. Some of the small specialized reissue labels, like Collector's Choice, sell the bulk of their releases through their own mail-order catalogs. Older record collectors who have an interest in reissue projects constitute the target market for catalogs from companies like Collector's Choice or Rediscover Music.

Other catalogs deal with specific genres of music, like jazz, polka music, or bluegrass. Mosaic Records is a jazz reissue label that operates entirely by selling albums through the mail.

How Distributors Operate

Distributors buy albums from a label and then sell them to retail stores. A CD with a list price of $15 costs the distributor about $7.50 and then gets sold to a retail store for a little over $10. Many of the distributors actively solicit sales with 800 numbers and faxes, and catalogs of the product that they have available.

One of the worst occurrences in the industry happens when an independent record distributor goes out of business. To put it simply, no one gets paid. The distributor goes into bankruptcy and a long list of people with unpaid bills appears. The records are not returned to the record company, which of course doesn't pay royalties to artists or songwriters, because the label hasn't been paid. One record company owner told me that when Bayside Distribution went out of business, they offered to sell his own labels' albums to him at a low price! Even worse, whatever bills are outstanding for records that have indeed been sold are never paid to the label. This is one of the most difficult aspects of running a small independent record label.

HOW RECORDS ARE SOLD TODAY

Selling records is a challenging and ever-changing scene in today's world. During the first half of the twentieth century, 78-rpm breakable records were the medium for records. Columbia Records introduced the long-playing (LP) record in 1948, ultimately triumphing over RCA's competing 7-inch 45-rpm format. Originally, the format for LPs was 10-inch albums for pop music and 12-inch albums for classical. The original LPs were monaural, but by 1958 stereo had taken over most of the business.

The reader needs to be aware that every time there has been a change of format, the record stores have been left with a good deal of unsold product that is virtually impossible to sell to the consumer. Further successful new formats have included the cassette tape and the CD, and unsuccessful formats included the 8-track tape, digital compact cassettes, and quadraphonic (four channel) records. It wasn't until the late 1980s that the CD finally become the dominant format for albums and, of course, there are still vinyl record enthusiasts who insist that their long-playing records sound better than compact discs.

Terry Currier revealed that during the 1985–1990 golden years of the record business, new product was easy to distribute to record stores. In addition to new recordings, many older albums were rereleased on CD, and many consumers bought these albums again to fit their new playback units. According to Terry, the average profit that a store realizes on a CD is currently about 31 percent, down about 5 percent over the past twenty years.

Terry also gives us a timeline on what has changed in the past twenty years about the method that artists and labels use to place product in chains and independent record stores:

> Let's go back to 1986. In 1986 the record industry was probably going into its peak time, for the first time in eight years, since the Fleetwood Mac *Rumours* and the Peter Frampton *Frampton Comes Alive* that were so successful. The CD had only been in existence for a couple of years but it was starting to take hold about 1986.
>
> The chain stores and the bigger box retailers were going through the metamorphosis of what to do, because they had LPs and cassettes in their stores, and they didn't have room for another medium, which was the CD.
>
> The major distribution companies at that time pretty much told all those people that CDs were going to be the current configuration of music and LPs would go away. Get rid of your LPs, because CDs are coming.
>
> They told them this because the industry CD sales were coming on like gangbusters. There was also more profit for the record companies on CDs than there were on LPs, because most of the LPs at that time were either $9.98 or $8.98 list. CDs were $14.98 or $15.98 at that time. So there was definitely going to be a little more profitability in the record companies for that.
>
> So what happened is, the major labels bought into that logic. The fact that the CD market was growing so quickly made it very

easy to get product into the stores. Business was growing in leaps and bounds from 1985 to 1990. Everyone seemed to be pretty profitable on the retail side, so everyone seemed to be open into bringing in new titles.

The reason the mall stores like Musicland had to eliminate one configuration is that rent was so high they couldn't make more room and pay more rent. There had to be some kind of reason for them to bring in those titles, whether it be getting radio airplay, someone was going to appear in a movie soundtrack, or other kinds of media attention. Or, it had to be a release by an artist who had a previous positive sales history.

As chains like Musicland developed, and as big box discount stores like Target and Best Buy entered the retail record business, several things transpired. The mall stores tended to carry fewer titles, and because of the high rent that they paid to the mall owners, titles needed to turn over quickly or the store would return them to the record company.

The other development was that some of the chains, especially Best Buy, heavily discounted CDs, using them as a loss leader to bring customers in to purchase refrigerators or televisions sets. This has made it more and more difficult for the independent retailer to compete with the chains.

Listening stations and end caps (end caps are displays at the end of a record bin) are also sources of income for both larger and independent stores. Terry Currier talks about some of these marketing techniques, and how artists and labels obtain that exposure for their product:

> In many cases, the label works with their distributor, and they say they want to do listening stations. The really savvy label may know stores up front, know what store is going to do well with that record in Chicago, Denver, etc. Then they go to that distributor and say they want to buy listening stations in those stores. When they don't know that stuff, then they have to rely upon the expertise of the distributor, and say, "Hey, I know that listening stations cost approximately this much per store, and I have a budget of $2000.00 to promote things in listening stations. Can you pick out and recommend stores?"
>
> If it's a label that is not distributed, the label will call the store direct, and see if they can set it up.
>
> A lot of labels on a real tight budget on the independent side may not have any budget at all for listening stations. They may get on the phone direct to the stores, and say, "Hey, I've got this really cool record I would like to send out to you. If you like it, let's set

something up and we can trade for some clean product." In other words, trading them the profit off a certain number of CDs for the listening station.

Or they may go to stores that they have good relationships with and ask if they have any discretionary listening booths. They could ask, "Could you just give me a slot if I send you a couple of CDs to put in your listening station?"

There are a lot of labels out there with no budget. When you go back to the sixties, one of the more expensive things in the record process was recording the record. Today, it can be the least expensive thing in the equation.

A listening station usually costs $50 per store. Some may charge $60, some may charge $35. I am talking about independent stores here. Now, Virgin Records in Times Square in New York might cost $300 to $400 per listening station because there is so much traffic.

There are other things record companies can buy in record stores. The only thing we sell at Music Millennium are listening stations, but in some record stores, they may sell every space of real estate in their store. A lot of the stores sell their window space, and even their wall space for promo posters. Even a lot of independents started doing that, because they saw the big box retailers were doing it.

I get other fellow retailers who tell me I should sell my window displays for $500 a pop. I don't agree with that; I want to promote what I want to promote, I don't want to sell those windows to the highest bidder.

In a Best Buy store, if you want your CD to be featured anywhere than the bin, it's going to cost you. If it's up on a bird feeder, up on a wall, on an end cap, its going to cost you.

Most of the independent retailers, unless they are of a sizeable strength, can't deal with the big box retailers in the first place. It's just too costly. Even if a Wal-Mart decides to take the product, unless there's a story to drive people in there (TV, radio, press) to the stores to buy those records, you are just going to see those records come back as returns.

The ideal situation is knowing what stores will be good at selling your albums, and give them any tools you can: in-store play copies, listening stations, and so forth.

We also should mention Wal-Mart, which allegedly sells about 10 percent of all the albums sold in this country. Not only does Wal-Mart have tremendous buying power, but it also may require artists to change album covers or even the lyrics of specific songs that the chain feels are not suitable for family listening or viewing. When Sheryl Crow recorded a song that discussed buying guns at Wal-Mart, the chain simply refused to carry that album. Interestingly enough, they continued to carry her earlier recordings.

The independent record stores have fought back by sponsoring more and more in-store performances by artists. These are free performances in the store, and are often keyed to a new CD being released or a traveling artist's local gig. It appears that the future of independent record stores is going to be increasingly tied to the notion of the store becoming an active entertainment center that is inviting to the consumer. The informality of this sort of performing environment also enables the consumer to talk to the artist or to get a CD autographed without being waylaid by a gang of security guards. Borders Books and Barnes & Noble are also sponsoring similar events, so it is not only the independent stores that are taking this approach.

I thought one of Terry Currier's more interesting observations about the state of the album retail marketing today, as opposed to twenty years ago, was the comparison in the way people view the intrinsic worth of music, then and now:

> One thing that is interesting is that the public perception of the worth of CDs and recorded music in general has changed. In 1986, LPs were $10.98, CDs were $14 to $15.98. Today's normal CD price is actually the same, $14 to $15.98. It's twenty years later. People thought they were a great value back then. People don't seem to have the same perception of the CD today as being a great value. You look at how other prices have doubled or tripled in that time on everything else, and it seems curious to me, despite the influence of free Internet downloads of music, etc.

TODAY'S OUTLOOK FOR THE ARTIST

As with so many things in the industry, there is good new and bad news. The good news is that the costs of making a recording continue to be smaller, and there are many opportunities to distribute music on the Internet, either by developing your own Web site or by using CD Baby or some of the other similar services. Digital sales constitute an ever-growing share of record sales, and there is every reason to expect this to continue. If you develop a Web site, it is essential that you make a commitment to placing new material on it periodically, or the consumer has no reason to return to your site. It is also important that you develop links to other compatible Web sites, so that you and your peers can share information about people interested in exploring compatible music styles.

Simply having a Web site places you in cyberspace along with hundreds of thousands, and eventually hundreds of millions of other people whose Web sites will unfortunately remain unknown to most music fans.

On the other hand, unauthorized digital downloading has had a variety of negative impacts on the careers of artists. First of all, there are the specific record sales that are lost, and the royalties that are in essence stolen from the artist. Perhaps even worse is the fact that the consumer becomes used to the notion of getting music free, and is therefore less inclined to buy CDs in the future.

There are several negative aspects to even legal digital downloads. On the one hand, most artists conceive of an album as a unified work, and the idea of someone ripping a single song or two from what the artist visualized as a coherent product is not pleasant. Imagine someone taking a single song off the Beatles' *Sergeant Pepper's* album or Brian Wilson's *Pet Sounds* masterpiece. Another aspect of downloading is that many consumers are listening to product on an iPod or similar listening device, with its miniature speakers of inferior quality. To an artist who has spent hours and hours trying to get the highest quality sound onto a CD, this has to represent a frustrating result. Inevitably, the quality of these portable devices is going to improve and that particular objection will go by the wayside. On the positive side, the fact that people will only download songs that they really want is likely to improve the general quality of songwriting.

5

THE EQUIPMENT YOU NEED TO DO THE JOB

There have been tremendous strides in the accessibility and price of instruments, guitars, recording equipment, PA systems, and associated gear over the past thirty-five years. Some elements necessary to a performing songwriter's ability to play songs have increased in price, while other tools have become cheaper. The Internet has made price comparisons easy, but as I talk about later in this chapter, I highly encourage songwriters/performers to buy from independent stores and develop a relationship with them whenever you can; it will be beneficial to both them and to you.

GUITARS

My first guitar was a Stella acoustic 6-string guitar, bought with money earned from my paper route in Omaha, Nebraska. It was essentially laminated softwoods with a painted fingerboard. After many hours of practice, that paint on the fret board wore off. That being said, I loved that guitar, and it became my ticket to adventure, travel, and romance.

In 1966, that guitar and case cost about $40. In today's dollars, that would equate to more than $200. The choices available for a beginning guitar today (2007) at that $200 price are many and varied, and they all have superior construction and tone in comparison to my beloved old Stella.

I think every songwriter has a special place in his heart for that first instrument that set him on that musical path. Eliza Gilkyson always wrote songs. She first played autoharp in a little folk duo with her sister. Growing up in Southern California, she had a unique source for guitars when she was ready for that step:

Myself and Carson VanDyke (VanDyke Parks's brother; renowned L.A. studio musician and producer) when down to Tijuana, Mexico, and picked up twelve good guitars in a shop that was selling tourist guitars. He gave me and my sisters the two nicest ones.

Then my dad took me to Wallach's Music City, at Sunset and Vine in Hollywood, and got me a Goya gut-string guitar. I gave it to my brother, who sold it to someone. Twenty-five years later, someone handed it back to me at one of my shows in Florida. It was a wonderful moment. My dad gave me that guitar and it was very meaningful to have it back. I used it on the title cut "Paradise Motel" of my most recent CD.

Some of the reasonably priced guitars in that beginning price range today, assuming you are not close to the Mexican border, are Alvarez, Washburn, Yamaha, and various brands by the Canadian maker Godin. These are excellent starter instruments, and there are a number of other manufacturers producing playable, decent-sounding starter guitars.

For serious songwriters and performers, Martin and Gibson remain the standard, with Taylor also becoming a very popular nameplate in the past fifteen years. I personally use a 1970 Martin D-28 and 1990 D-41 as my 6-string choices, and use a 1970 Martin D-12-35 and 1965 Gibson B-45-12 as my 12-string workhorses.

Gordon Lightfoot has his signature Gibson 12-string and Martin 6-string guitars that he uses on stage, with a slightly different twist.

I have two 1960s pin bridge Gibson B-45 12-string guitars. One of them is tuned to an open D capoed in the third position, which gives me that open D chord [in the key of F]. I call it the F-12. The other one is tuned straight, with the capo on the second fret, and it never gets moved. I stopped moving that capo years ago. If you try to move it onstage the guitar goes out of tune.

I've been using a 6-string D-18 for a long time, but I have got a brand new one that I got made after Martin guitars did the Gordon Lightfoot series [Martin made sixty-one specially ornamented, signed guitars by Gordon in 1999]. I gave one of them to one of my kids, so I got them to make me one, and that's the one I am using right now. It is really accurate. I've been working on my tuning a lot too, so we are winning that battle.

Those guitars are the tools of my trade.

Aside from the Martins and Gibsons that Lightfoot favors, there are dozens, if not hundreds, of independent makers. All across North America, there are hundreds of independent luthiers (guitar makers) who produce superb instruments that rival or exceed the guitars of those major manufacturers. If you are interested in these sorts of guitars, ask your fellow musicians and local luthiers about brands they know and respect, and sample those guitars as you are able. Some of the most popular smaller guitar makers are Collings, Larivie, and Santa Cruz, but there are many reputable artisans turning out instruments of amazing quality, each instrument with its own unique sound. Expect to pay between $3000 to a much higher price for these boutique instruments.

The guitar, along with the piano, has become the gold standard for songwriters because of its complete scale, chordal possibilities, prevalence in popular music, and its three octaves, but countless songs are also written and performed on mandolin, fiddle, accordion, and other more unusual and even unique instruments. Only a few short years ago, it was very difficult to find a bouzouki or an octave mandolin to play your songs, if that was the sound you desired for them. With the propagation of Celtic music, African music, and other blends of sounds from around the world, today there are instrument makers easily accessible that seem to cater to almost every musical need that you can think of, with a simple Internet inquiry.

Harry Manx helped make his reputation with a truly unique instrument, the Mohan Veena from India. It was truly a fascinating musical journey for Manx to hear and find this instrument, and the person who taught it to him. In Manx's case, that unique instrument and his mastery of it has been a major component of his success. I first heard Manx play this instrument at the Juan De Fuca Music Festival in 2002, and people were spellbound by its unique sound and appearance. Though I have been performing myself at festivals for more than thirty years, I had never seen such an instrument. I asked Manx how he ever came about such an unusual conveyance for his songs.

> I actually went to India for the first time in 1979. I was in Europe, and hitchhiked most of the way to India. I ended up going through Iran, and getting caught in the revolution, getting into Pakistan, and finally into India. I spent a year there just hanging around, traveling around, bought a sitar, and learned to play a little bit.
>
> I had always wanted to go back, so I went back in 1986, with the idea that I would just stay there. I had set myself up in Japan to be able to make money, to go over there and play a few shows, to busk on the street.

So I took an apartment there in India, and this time I said, "I'm going to dig in deep," and find out what it is about the music and the spiritual aspect of the country that I love so much.

I met my teacher, Vishwa Mohan Bhatt, at his home, but I had heard a recording of one of his CDs when I was over in Japan doing some shows. It was funny that I heard about him in Japan, and not in India. So I was just passing a little record shop in Japan and they were playing it. So I went in and said, "What's that?" They didn't have a picture of his instrument on the cover [the Mohan Veena] but I heard a sitar and a slide guitar, both of the things that I am interested in. I was looking through the CD booklet when I saw a picture of it and realized it was one instrument that did both.

As soon as I got back to India, I phoned up a few musicians I knew in New Delhi. They gave me his phone number. I called him, and he was living in Rahjastan, about 2000 kilometers from where I was living, south of Bombay. I told him I was a slide player, living in India, and was there any chance I could come and meet him? He said to come, and I arrived at his place late in the evening. He was still awake, and he invited me in. I had my guitar, and his son had arranged for me to have a hotel. He asked me what I played; he had not met a lot of Westerners that played slide guitar. So I played a few things for him. He got his Mohan Veena out then, and just kind of strummed it with a flourish. Then, I knew I was toast. I wasn't going anywhere.

I would do anything, say anything, to be there with him. I didn't want to overwhelm him with that feeling, so I kept it to myself. But I was there the next morning, at 8 A.M., with my guitar. He was surprised to see me, but I asked to see the Mohan Veena again. He said to me later on that day, "I think you should stay here and play." He went over and took another Mohan Veena off of the wall, handed it to me, and said, "You can play this one here. Take it to your hotel and practice." A few days later, I phoned up my friends where I had been living, and asked them to send my stuff to me, because I wasn't coming back.

I stayed with him for five years. We traveled around India, and his sons, who are also fine players, also helped me to learn the instrument. I became Vishwa's good friend, and it was a lovely journey for me.

I just let myself travel that road for a number of years, and I felt very content there. I felt no need to be anywhere else—like there was so much there, and so much to discover. I wasn't even ready to leave when I did in 1998, but my teachers encouraged me. They said, "Use what you know, and it will get just that much better. If you just stay a student all of your life, learning the instrument, it is not doing anybody any good, so get out there and use it."

Harry Manx returned to Canada in 1999, and indeed began to use what he had learned in India.

Pickups for Acoustic Guitars

It wasn't so many years ago that using a Shure SM-57 to mike an acoustic guitar was the standard professional setup. In a quiet, solo, concert setting, using a microphone on the guitar is still my preferred method (though today I would use a different microphone). Unfortunately, if you are performing with your guitar for a living, the chances are that those concert situations will be in the minority of what you do as a musician.

Many acoustic guitars today, particularly those by Takamine, come with preinstalled electronics and equalizers so you can plug right into the PA. Eliza Gilkyson is very partial to the total sound that her Takamine produces.

> I have to say I am really in love with my Takamine. It has a great graphic EQ system in it, and it can handle that C tuning I use for many of my songs. I can go in and out of the C tuning, and very few guitars can do that. The neck is great, and it is perfect for me. It is really easy to work, with low action, and it has a big sound. However, when I am at home I play old Gibsons and parlor guitars.

Many of the more established brands, like Martin, prefer to sell their guitars as a totally acoustic instrument, and the owners need to pay to put a pickup into them if they choose to go that route.

The reasons guitar pickups have become almost standard in stage acoustic guitars are many. Many performing situations are noisy, and if you turn up the instrument microphone level enough for you to be heard, you will most likely have problems with feedback. If the acoustic guitar is being used in a band situation, you can adjust the volume up without needing to be concerned about the other instruments volume bleeding into the guitar microphone, which again invites feedback. It is also much more accurate to adjust the tone and volume of your guitar with the band mix if you have a pickup.

If you need to install a pickup in your acoustic guitar, expect to spend between $100 and $400 for the pickup itself, then another $75 to

$200 to have it professionally installed. I highly recommend you have an experienced guitar repair person you know do this. The installer will be drilling holes in your precious instrument, and you want someone who is skilled to do this. Also, with most acoustic guitar pickups, the exact placement of the pickup determines the quality of the reproduced sound of your guitar.

If you are on a concert or festival stage, you will also need what is called a "direct input box" (or DI box, as it is commonly referred to) to match impedance between your guitar signal and the PA. These are also useful to get a quality guitar sound through any PA system. Most festivals and soundmen have direct boxes, though the quality varies. Some direct input boxes are of simple design. Others, such as the L. R. Baggs direct boxes I use, are complex preamps, with input, volume, tone, treble, and feedback controls built in. Expect to pay as little as $50 to as much as $240 for a good direct input box.

I recommend you invest in a good quality direct input box, to complement the guitar pickup you choose. The combination of both pieces of gear produces a superior sound for stringed instruments when amplification is needed.

With an instrument like the Mohan Veena, or even the lap slide guitar, it is tricky to get a good sound even with a pickup. Harry Manx is known for the quality stage sound of his instruments, and talks a little bit about how he gets that big sound:

> I use a B-Band system from Scandinavia for the Mohan Veena. It picks up the strings and gives it a very full sound; I am very impressed with it.
>
> For the 6-string lap slide guitar, I use a Taylor with a Sunrise pickup. I'm a big fan of the Sunrise.
>
> To get the sound I am after for the guitars through the PA, I use a rack with Pre-Sonus preamps, then I use a Mackie mixer. I then give the house a line out of the Mackie. I also run my own speakers out of that board, except for vocals—that way I can avoid getting a lot of instrument feedback and getting a different sound every night. I just bring my own instrument monitors and that takes care of that.
>
> I always wanted to play through good preamps on stage, because I know that is what gives you that warmth of sound in the studio. I tried a lot of different ones, and I found the Pre-Sonus are the best ones for me. They warm up the tone and clarity of the instrument about 50 percent more than you would normally get, so I really rely on those.

A lot of acoustic guitarists don't bother with that kind of outboard gear; they just plug into a direct box and go with that. The difference is that folks that come to my show, they hear this huge big sound, with bass ... without the loud volume. It is a fullness that comes through, without having a band, and I can say that is all about having those Pre-Sonus preamps.

I play with my fingers directly on the strings; I don't use any picks. I love the sound of just the notes, no sound of any steel hitting the strings. I can do a lot more with just my fingers than I could do with picks.

Guitar Strings

It has thankfully been decades now since the only strings that were available outside of a major city were the Black Diamond brand. There has been an exponential increase in the kinds of guitar strings available since the late 1970s. The 1980s saw the advance of phosphor-bronze coatings, which significantly increases string life and makes for a bright, crisp sound. In the 1990s, the W. L. Gore & Associates corporation developed a different coating that they called Polyweb for their Elixir brand strings. This coating makes their strings last longer than any other commercially available guitar strings, though some players found the sound somewhat less animated than they preferred. In response to that criticism, they now also make a Nanoweb coating string that has a brighter sound, but still keeps its sound much longer than traditional guitar strings.

With an aggressive endorsement, festival sponsorship, and ad campaign, Elixir has captured a significant segment of the stringed instrument market. Elixir strings are significantly more expensive but also last much longer. Expect to pay $15 to $20 for Elixir strings, less online and in quantity.

Every guitar player, or string player of any kind, has his own style of attack on the strings, his own body chemicals, and his own unique environment that the strings are used in. This, along with the kind of string used, will determine how long the string lasts.

All of these factors play a part in both the sound and the satisfaction that the guitar player has in his or her strings, and the only way to discover this is by trying many different brands until you find what you are happy with.

Most professional performing songwriters will change strings once they sound "dead" to them, but not all. Chuck Pyle, a well-known Colorado and national performer, prefers strings that are very well used, to give his bass finger-style notes a certain kind of "chunk" to them that is part of his sound.

Many string players prefer the D'Addario brand, which has a long and storied history. They will cost between $8 and $11, and less than that when ordered in quantity.

Some other popular and reputable string makers are Ernie Ball, Martin, and Dean Markley, and there are many other brands to experiment with, as well.

Mail Order and Internet Catalog Sites

For all of the instruments and equipment discussed in this chapter, there are many options when you decide to purchase. Up until the late 1980s, a musician was pretty well confined to a physical music store for his professional needs, but the Internet has changed all of that. I have listed just a few online and catalog distributors below.

On the other hand, never underestimate a real connection to a local music shop for purchasing your instruments and musical supplies. Most independently owned shops have become much more competitive in price, out of necessity, with the national chains and Web sites, and you will receive superior service from your local shop in most cases. You also will be able to physically sample the instrument or the piece of gear you will, in most cases, own for years to come.

Certain kinds of recording equipments will be had at a cheaper price at some of the musical big box stores, but if you are unfamiliar with how to use the gear, or need repairs on the equipment, it will be problematic for you if you purchased the equipment at such a place. A good friend of mine works at a small store that specializes in high-end microphones and recording gear, such as Pro Tools setups, which has become the standard of the industry for home recording. He frequently has calls from folks who bought their Pro Tools recording units online or at a big box store for a bargain basement price. When they find they don't understand how to use the equipment, and the place they bought it from doesn't have any idea how to use it either, they call him. He has to tell them that he can't help them, and that they need to call the place where they bought the equipment from (which is who they have just called, and who does not have any idea how to help them with nasty little problems like interface issues). At that point, the Pro Tools customer is going to need to invest many hours in finding out the proper procedures by researching Web sites, calling people he or she knows who might have answers to the problems, or going to a paid seminar where someone can translate the word jumble that is the online owner's manual.

For those customers, they need at that point to invest $50 to $100 an hour to try to learn from a pro to how get the equipment they bought to work for them.

If they had bought the Pro Tools setup from a reputable small business instead of the big box store, unlimited advice and guidance is generally available.

Also, with purchases from a big box store, repair service is contracted out to outside firms or back to the manufacturer, generally taking a much longer period of time than going through an independent retailer.

The owners of a local music store also tend to be generous with their patrons about scuttlebutt on gigs available in the area, new products the owners themselves use, and other musical opportunities for performing singer/songwriters. It can be a lonely world out there for someone trying to do this as a living; taking advantage of the ready-made communities like those that exist in independent music stores can be good for both the soul and the wallet.

Some independent music stores, such as Artichoke Music in Portland, Oregon, will even offer their customers a plethora of information and opportunities such as:

- Instruction in mainstream instruments, and unusual ones too, such as the dobro and Celtic-style fiddle.
- Chances to meet well-known songwriters and interact with them at small-sized workshops.
- Opportunities to sing and perform their own songs on stage in special student situations.

All of that being said, many folks are not in an area where a full-service music store is available. Here are three reputable phone/Internet retailers that have good reputations.

Elderly Instruments in East Lansing, Michigan, bills itself as the world's largest Martin guitar distributor, which they are. They also have a huge assortment of other well-known and not-so-well-known guitars, banjos, mandolins, and just about any other musical device or accessory you can think of. They have a series of catalogs you can subscribe to, a wonderful Web site, and a newsletter Web site devoted entirely to vintage instruments. They are worth a visit in person to their store in East Lansing, Michigan, or a cyberstop to buy or educate yourself on prices, models, and brands (www.elderly.com).

Musician's Friend is an Internet/mail-order business based out of Medford, Oregon. They have an incredible array of instruments, PA gear, recording equipment, and accessories. Their pricing is very competitive.

In my dealings with them through the years, they have been fair and honest, with prompt customer service (www.musiciansfriend.com).

Sweetwater has a vast selection of acoustic and electric instruments, and one of the larger electronic keyboard selections online. They also sell the complete Pro Tools recording line, high-end microphones, and PA gear (www.Sweetwater.com).

PIANOS

In the mid-1970s, the Yamaha Company brought out the first "portable" piano with weighted keys that actually sounded something like a real piano. Unfortunately, "portable" still required a furniture dolly or very strong band members. Also, like a real piano, it required tuning each time it was moved. This instrument retailed for between $1500 and $2000 when it was new, which was a lot of money in those days.

Silicon chips soon changed everything in the electronic keyboard world. Yamaha, Korg, Roland, and Kurzweil all developed portable keyboards of reasonable weight that featured weighted keys, at least a 66-keyboard scale, and ever-improving piano sounds.

For the songwriter/composer, these keyboards today are remarkable tools that allow you to write and print music through your computer, to use it as a recorder for your musical thoughts, to arrange entire scores in both the bass and treble clefs for various instrumental ranges, and many more tasks.

I would venture to say that nothing has ever changed the composing/arranging world as much as the digital keyboard has, over the period of a short twenty years.

For the singer/songwriter/performer, these keyboards begin at remarkably affordable prices, starting with practice keyboards at $100 or less. For stage pianos, expect to pay between $500 and $4000 for a truly mind-boggling array of sounds and features. Roland, Alesis, and Yamaha still make wonderful instruments all across the price spectrum; look to Nord, Electro, and Hammond for some of the professionals' choices.

PA SYSTEMS

My first PA system was a Peavey, bought in about 1973. I was a performer who still played clubs, yet also did concerts and aspired to do more of those, and there was quite a debate in the folksinger/songwriter community at that time about whether having a PA system was "selling out." The argument was, if you had a PA, you would be tempted to play more clubs and neglect the more respected "artistic and meaningful" world of folk concerts and coffeehouses.

The fact is, I never had any problem working in both worlds. If anything, having to deal with loud barroom crowds full of people who weren't there to hear me was great training in learning to be an entertainer, talking to the crowds, and getting them involved in some way with what you do. Those lessons are valuable no matter the performing situation you find yourself in, whether it is a wedding reception or Carnegie Hall.

As a performing singer/songwriter trying to get gigs, every advantage you can give yourself in being saleable is important. Having a quality PA system with good microphones and that you can haul and set up easily is an important component of being a singer/songwriter/performer—particularly when you are just starting out. The flexibility and marketability it gives you will far outweigh the cost of the PA and the aggravation of loading, unloading, and setting it up.

When you reach the touring level that the performers interviewed in this book have achieved, you are generally ensured of at least an adequate PA and a competent soundman. Still, Gordon Lightfoot brings his own soundman with him, and many touring artists working at that concert level do that same.

In the field of music I am in, there are still a number of traveling singer/songwriter/performers who do not carry a PA with them on their driving tours.

Though it is true the PA takes up space, and is something you have to consider might be stolen; I have never understood not bringing one with me on an extended tour (unless I am flying to all the dates, as I often have had to do).

Years ago, I played at the Dodge County Fair in Nebraska, who assured me they had an excellent PA and told me I would not have to bring my own. When I arrived with my band, it was a dismal sounding antique of a PA. Still, the organizers somehow enjoyed the concert, and invited me back the following year, this time assuring me they had a new, wonderful PA.

When my band and I arrived that day, we found the new system they had touted to me was a Fender guitar amplifier. Fortunately, I had hauled my PA with me this time, just in case, and was able to sound good amidst the hot dog vendors and fire engine bells. Having the PA with you gives you the ability to at least reach baseline respectability in your sound, no matter the situation.

Harry Manx has played in hundreds of different performance situations, from a street corner in Japan to sold-out concert halls in Australia. When we were chatting and I asked if he ever got frustrated with the sound variances, he said,

> When I show up, and the PA system doesn't have subwoofers [for the PA bass fullness], I find I lose a lot of the tone that I am putting out. I like to fill up the whole room with the sound spectrum. So any time those subs are missing, I find that a bit frustrating.
>
> These days I tend to play in places that have great PA systems. I'm not carrying a soundman anymore, though I did for a few years. So when things do go wrong, it's a great opportunity to be creative!
>
> I'm not a star up there. When something goes wrong, I look at my audience and say, "This is really screwed up—you can see it, I can see it. Just give me a minute, OK?"

Sometimes in this business you are amazed at the PA situation you find yourself in, no matter what your preparations or expectations are. In 1999 I did a number of opening acts at the Nebraska State Fair in Lincoln for big-name country artists. My final opening act of that extended gig was on Labor Day 1999, in the Bob Devaney Sports Arena at 2 P.M. I was to open a sold-out concert in front of 12,000 fans for the country-rock group Alabama. No big deal, I said to myself, I had opened for many similar kinds of shows throughout my career.

What I didn't realize until I showed up for the sound check was that Alabama had taken out the arena's monitor board and amplifier, and replaced it with their own board to run their in-the-ear-monitor system.

The result of this was that I had no monitors. For a big show like that in a sports arena, the main speakers are generally hung in front of you and about 20 feet above you. The sports arena was built like a giant upside-down bowl. Hence, the only sound I could hear on stage, as I played and sang my songs, was the echo of my voice and guitar off the back walls, with a delay of about half a second or more.

This was distracting, difficult, and unfulfilling, to say the least. However, I knew how the songs *felt* under my fingers on the fret board after so many years, and so I concentrated on ignoring what I heard and listening to my voice acoustically. The audience seemed to enjoy my songs and was very kind, and I never mentioned on stage that I felt as if I were singing in a really big ceramic bathroom. In a situation like that, you do what you need to do as well as you can do it, collect the paycheck, and hope the next gig is better!

Yes, most concert halls and some clubs have their own PAs and soundmen, some of them good, others not. I have had numerous performances, even in respected venues, that I have simply endured because of bad sound, with no recourse to correct it.

When I asked Gordon Lightfoot if a bad PA had ever ruined one of his performances, he said,

> The only performance that was ever ruined was when I was taken suddenly drunk in London, England, in 1980. It wasn't the equipment's fault. I can't recall ever having done a bad show for that reason. I remember working with bad sound systems, but never to the point where you could not do the performance.

Well, there is that substance danger too, which most professional musicians have fallen prey to some time in our careers, and eventually learned to deal with if we manage to stay in the business (or stay alive) very long.

When I need to provide my own PA, I currently use a Mackie 808S stereo powered mixer, able to power both mains and monitors with a reasonable amount of power. I use JBL Eon speakers on speaker stands. The Eons are lightweight, only about 23 pounds apiece, and sound good. This PA is adequate in a small to medium club setting of 50 to 150 people, and in concert hall setting of up to about 300. The total cost for these three essential pieces (powered mixer, two speakers) is around $1200 to $1500 depending on where you buy them.

For years the standard of the club/small concert performers was the Shure Vocalmaster system. The speakers were over 5 feet tall, and incredibly heavy. The powered mixer was also very heavy, and the entire system was very bassey with very little clarity, particularly for the vocalist. That system cost over $1000, a lot of money (and a lot of weight to carry) back then. For the sake of my fifty-three-year-old body, I am thankful for not only the vast increase in the sound quality of modern PAs but also for the decreased weight of the systems.

JBL remains one of the leaders in festival and theater-quality speakers, and also in PA speakers for the hobbyist, church, and professional traveling troubadours. Many seasoned performing veterans and organizations also swear by the Mackie SRM350 speakers, which have a power amp built into the speaker itself. This means you don't need an amplifier built into the mixer, but rather just a mixing board, which is a much cheaper piece of gear. You will, however, need a separate amplifier if you want/need to run stage monitors too. I have sung through many of these Mackie speakers, and they do sound great.

The Mackie SRM350s retail at $700 each, but can be had for about $550 to $650. These are the choice of many smaller touring groups and medium-size concert venues today, and the sound quality is excellent.

Other dependable names in PA gear include Peavey, Yamaha, Kustom, Behringer, and Bose. Also, Fender makes its Passport series, featuring very light components, suitable for small venues, which runs from $400 to $850, complete with mikes, speaker stands, mike cords, clips, and so on.

I believe the rule of thumb for PAs and any other gear talked about in this chapter is to buy the very best you can afford at the time. You do yourself no favor by purchasing inferior equipment that does not showcase your songs and your talent to its best advantage.

MICROPHONES

Aside from the choice of your primary songwriting/performing instrument (piano, guitar, etc.), there is no more crucial link in the chain of communicating your song to the listener than the microphone you choose.

The best-selling microphones for decades now have been the Shure SM-57 (used primarily for instrument recording) and the Shure SM-58 (used primarily for voice).

These microphones are workhorses, and still offer decent sound replication for a very reasonable price; right around $100 will buy you either of these. They have good feedback rejection and are virtually indestructible.

Eliza Gilkyson has very strong opinions about the Shure SM-57s and 58s, which she shares with her songwriting classes:

> I actually just want to put the word out there that people need to get rid of the Shure SM-58s on their voice. I think that is just the worst mike. In my songwriter workshops, I teach microphone technique. I actually set people up with a Shure SM-57, an SM-58, and my Shure Beta 58. I set everything flat on the mixing board, and have people walk through and try these mikes and see the difference.
>
> There is only perhaps one in twenty people who the SM-58 will work for with those flat settings. I think if people would switch over to the Shure Beta mikes, that would solve a lot of problems.
>
> The Shure Beta 57 mike is a great mike to travel with, because it is not a $600 microphone. It's a great workhorse that a regular musician can afford and travel with.

I think that people just have to A-B test the mikes and find what works for them. I have a big midrange voice and I have kind of an upper mid honk that the Beta 57 smoothed out for me. I don't have a typical voice, though, and people really just need to see what works for them.

I used a Shure SM-57 and SM-58 combination all through the 1970s. At that time, guitar pickups were in their infancy and didn't sound very good, and there just weren't a lot of choices available in the performing microphone world.

In the 1980s I became very fond of the Audio Technica microphones for guitar miking on stage, and used an ATM-31 for that purpose for many years before I began using pickups in my guitars. That Audio Technica microphone is still in my bag, and is often useful if I need extra miking capability for some reason.

If you are a singer, and most songwriters are, there are great microphones in a variety of price ranges available today to make your voice sound as good as it possibly can when you perform your songs. I highly encourage you to sample some of these microphones I mention, find one that is complimentary to your voice, buy it, and take it to all of your gigs. You will then be working with a microphone you know the characteristics of, as well as a microphone that has not been abused by hundreds of singers, soundmen, and other various reprobates.

One important side benefits of always taking and using your own microphone if you are playing a lot of gigs is, that you will find yourself contracting fewer colds. In many performing situations such as festivals and open mikes, you often will be using a microphone minutes after another person has sung through it. The health risks are obvious, and there is nothing more uncomfortable or debilitating for a singer than a nasty head cold.

My bass player, Donny Wright, often has people ask if they can borrow his stage microphone (an Audio Technica AE-5400, an excellent vocal mike) to sing through when he is taking a break. His standard response is, "You can use my mike and give it back to me, if I can borrow your toothbrush and then give it back to you."

I know that my voice is my major stock in trade, and I have come to believe over the years that money spent on a voice microphone is well spent, indeed. I currently use an Audix VX-10 on stage. It is the best stage mike I have ever used, with a rich midrange, wonderful responsiveness when I move off the mike a little, and a clarity and depth that is the best I have ever experienced. It retails for $600, and can be had for between $450 and $525.

Neumann is a legend in recording microphones, and a few years ago entered their microphone in the high-performing sweepstakes: the KMS-105. Harry Manx uses one of these. It has similar characteristics to the Audix VX-10, though the Audix has a much higher gain ratio (the power signal that comes from the microphone itself). The Neumann KMS-105 retails for $850, but again is discounted significantly through a number of stores and dealers. Both the Audix and the Neumann (and many other of the microphones described here) require true 48-volt phantom power on your mixing board to run. This is a fairly standard feature today on most boards, but it is always a good idea to check with the soundman in advance to make sure his mixer has this feature, if you are using one of these mikes. I also carry a good-quality dynamic microphone, in the unlikely event there is no phantom power on the mixing board.

AKG makes an excellent vocal microphone with a high gain response, the AKG 535B. I own one of these, and take it with me when I travel by airplane. They sound great, but do not have the creamy midrange of the Audix or the Neumann, at least for my voice. They retail for $462 and usually can be bought for around $300 or less.

As Eliza Gilkyson mentioned, Shure has also upgraded its entire line with their Beta series. The Beta series features superior electronics and feedback rejection, plus significant clarity response, to their standard 57 and 58 models. I have not used any of the Shure Beta series microphones myself, but Eliza and many other performers rave about them.

On the rare occasion that I need to use an instrument microphone, I have an AKG C-1000. These have great frequency response for a variety of instruments for stage use, and usually are available for around $200 or less.

RECORDING EQUIPMENT, PRO TOOLS, AND SO ON

With the advent of less expensive, quality recording equipment in the late 1970s, many singer/songwriters chose to set up home studios to record their own songs. In those days, a home recording setup might have consisted of a 4-track Tascam reel-to-reel tape machine, a mixing board, and a couple of Shure microphones.

The technology of the new century has made the home-recording option ever more appealing, and the array of excellent recording systems, microphones, and other gear available to the musician who wants to make his or her own CDs is mind boggling.

However, before you make your first album and go to trick out a complete home studio, begin by acquainting yourself with some of the basics of how recordings are done. For around $300 to $500, you can pick up a basic 8-track hard disc recorder that allows you to record, overdub, and mix your own multitrack projects. Working with a unit like this is invaluable experience when you move on to bigger projects and other studios, and you will always be able to use it for demos and basic recordings. Tascam and Fostex both make basic units that have an amazing array of features for such reasonable prices.

Most of the Internet/mail-order outlets mentioned earlier in this chapter have recording "packages" available, consisting of microphones, recording device, stands, and speakers. Again, I highly suggest you visit with someone who actually has her own recording setup, and find out what her experience has been with some of this gear. While some of it works very well, some of it can be difficult and complicated to operate, and may not interface well with other components you may already own.

Also, if you find an audio store with a knowledgeable proprietor or employee, their assistance is invaluable, both before and after the sale of the gear, as I wrote about earlier in the chapter.

The Pro Tools recording solution by Digidesign has become an affordable standard for both home recorders and many professional studios. It utilizes totally digital technology to track, edit, and mix your songs, using your computer to visually edit and mix. Pro Tools recording setups begin at $500 for a simple M-Box and go up in price exponentially, depending on the complexity and number of tracks desired in the system. You do have to have a computer new enough and sophisticated enough to handle the Pro Tools information. Most Pro Tools setups tend to work best on Mac computers, though the program will run on regular PCs as well. If you decide to go this route for your recordings, make sure you have help; it is more complicated to record this way than it may seem in the demos, and the learning curve is steep. That being said, it is a wonderful solution to songwriters' desires to record themselves whenever they please, without having to always pay studio charges.

There is a new clearinghouse for musician reviews, latest gear, techs and tutorials, and other services that has just been set up on the Internet. It is called www.harmony-central.com. It looks as if it will be a valuable resource to compare the quality of brands of technical equipment before you actually buy, and to help you figure it out after you get it home. Still, I believe nothing takes the place of being able to pick up the phone and call a reputable independent dealer, and get your questions answered by a live human being. Anyone who has tried to decipher the instructions to fix a computer problem knows this is so, and figuring out how to get some of this highly technical equipment to interface and work is equally difficult without personal support.

6

NEXT STEPS
Moving Forward

THE IMPORTANCE OF FESTIVALS AND SONGWRITING COMPETITIONS IN A COMPOSER'S CAREER

Festivals

Music festivals are an important and gratifying part of a performer's career. At a music festival, you usually reach a large number of people who are interested in hearing your music, people who you would not normally connect with on the club level. You also have excellent opportunities to sell CDs and other products to a diverse audience and build your fan base.

Festivals are many and varied in format, pay, and amenities for performers. I have performed at dozens of them, and directed many of them as well, which gives me an interesting perspective on the joys and frustrations about being involved with such events.

Some of the major songwriters' festivals that take place in North America each year are the Vancouver Folk Festival in Vancouver, British Columbia; Falcon Ridge in Connecticut; the Winnipeg Folk Festival in Winnipeg, Manitoba; and the Kerrville Folk Festival in Kerrville, Texas. These are big events, with multiple stages and attendance that numbers in the tens of thousands of people.

There are other, smaller festivals that emphasize a variety of music and songwriters, such as the Juan De Fuca Festival in Port Angeles,

Washington; the Sisters Folk Festival in Sisters, Oregon; and the Rocky Mountain Folks Festival in Lyons, Colorado.

Bluegrass and blues festivals are really their own subcategory, with literally hundreds of them taking place across the United States each year. Some feature very traditional bluegrass music, while others are more open to different styles (such as the Telluride Bluegrass Festival, which features its own Troubadour songwriting competition).

As a general rule, most bluegrass festivals emphasize tradition over composition, though again there are notable exceptions to that rule. Most regions have bluegrass associations that can fill you in on the details of the festivals in your area. Similarly, blues festivals are often sponsored by regional blues organizations.

There are thousands of other smaller festivals that incorporate music into their format that take place in small towns and big cities, in muddy farm fields and suburban concrete parking lots. These are often excellent opportunities for newer singer/songwriters to reach a festival audience.

There are also a few festivals along the line of the Seattle Folklife Festival, which takes place each May in Seattle. Performers there have 17 minutes to play their music, and there is no pay involved, only a token compensation for travel. The festival has a huge attendance of over 100,000 people per year (attendance is free for the public), but it has set disturbing precedents in the way it treats its performers and sells their products. The competition for a venue to perform in this business is such that they regularly turn musicians away, even though they may have applied for a performing slot months in advance. The festival staff is paid, and generally a featured ensemble from overseas has its expenses paid. The rest of the money donated by the enthusiastic crowds and the grants that are procured goes toward administrative costs and the rental of Seattle Center for that weekend. The performers also pay the festival a significant commission on the CDs they sell there.

The Seattle Folklife Festival is a great party and a celebration of many diverse styles of music and dance, but I think it benefits the listeners and amateur songwriter/performers much more than any aspiring or practicing professionals who play their songs there. On the other hand, an event like this can be an invaluable experience in networking with other musicians, and you truly never know who might be listening to you.

You can consult with a number of regional guides to find out about music festivals and other sorts of festivals in your geographic area that you can apply to.

In the Pacific Northwest (Washington, Oregon, Idaho, and Montana), you can subscribe to *Festivals Directory Northwest,* which costs $55 for a one-year, four-issue subscription. This is a comprehensive guide that gives you events, dates, number of stages, type of music booked in previous years, and so forth (www.festivalsdirectory.com).

Ontario, Canada, has a long tradition of music festivals, and has its own music festival association at www.festivalsandeventsontario.ca.

Sing Out! magazine has an upcoming festival listing at the back of each issue, as does *Dirty Linen* magazine. Each magazine listing has all the contact information, Web site, and artists that are booked for this year's festival. Both magazines' Web sites and subscription information are listed in the Musicians' Resources section of the bibliography.

There are other publications that list festivals of all kinds months in advance, such as *Bluegrass Unlimited, Living Blues,* state and regional AAA guides, *Sunset Magazine,* and various geographic tour guides that you might find in a hotel room when you are visiting an area.

I try to always keep a little memo notebook with me when I am traveling, and write down any interesting festivals that I think I might fit into, for future reference. I have actually booked a number of festivals in this fashion, including the Rapid City (South Dakota) Heritage Days Festival, the Tumbleweed Festival in Garden City, Kansas, and a few others.

What kind of materials do you need to get hired to play a festival? The standard answer for being booked anywhere remains true here, with a few extra additions and considerations.

- The promotional package for this type of gig does not need to be extensive, but it does have to be high quality. I once had a major Canadian festival director tell me he does not look at more than one write-up review from the performer's hometown; reviews from other places where that performer was unknown are much more important to him. The CD that is enclosed with the promo package should include some live performance material.
- If you have performed at other festivals, be sure to include letters of recommendation from the festival director. Make sure these letters include commentary on your interaction with the audience, and preferably comment on your professionalism (showing up on time, being willing to fit within time parameters, etc.). Make sure each letter has a phone number, so the director who is considering hiring you can just pick up the phone and talk to the person who has worked with you before. If you do not have letters like this in your festival promo package and you have successfully worked in festivals before, get them!
- A Web site is a must. Festival directors are busy people and want to be able to access your site immediately to answer any

questions they may have about your biography and current tour schedule. They also like to be able to easily harvest promo pictures and other material from your site when they need it.

- As when booking other kinds of gigs, first call and introduce yourself and tell the director or secretary you will be sending along a package. After you do that, follow-up calls within a reasonable period of time are advised. Don't get discouraged; for desirable festivals, you may have to apply for many years before you get your foot in the door. Be sure to make clear you are available to do workshops, school programs, and whatever other festival music duties you feel you can contribute.

If you are in the town or area doing a gig where a festival will be held, call the festival office or director and invite him or her to come to your show. Remember, *nothing* is as effective a booking tool as the promoter, booker, or festival director seeing you perform live.

I have just accepted the post of being director of a new festival in Ocean Shores, Washington (the North Coast Folk Festival). All the performers that I have booked thus far for the festival have either been a guest on *River City Folk* or I have seen them perform live in front of an audience. As I mentioned earlier in the book, this is how you actually get the breaks you need to do this profession full time—by being seen, live, by the right people, by performing your songs at every opportunity. Talking to other festival booking people, I find that most of them feel the same way; they need to see the performer, or at least have a very strong recommendation from another director or booking person they respect, before they hire you.

Musicians have also worked their way onto festival stages by working as event volunteers, emcees, and offering to help with the dozens of tasks that need to be accomplished long before the first note of music is ever played for the festival audience. Don't get discouraged; be aware that moving from the club stage to a festival stage is a big jump, and it is not an easy one; for most performers, it requires perseverance, organization, and luck.

Eliza Gilkyson found booking festivals herself a daunting task.

I was never able to get into festivals until my agent, Val Denn, got me in. Kerrville was the only one I got into myself, and that was just because I was well known locally. Even then, I really only got booked at Kerrville regularly when I went onboard with Val.

I think it is very difficult to book without an agent. I don't think you are taken seriously, and I don't think promoters want to work with the artist. For the most part, artists aren't the best persons to do their own booking. They take things way too personally, and they don't represent themselves in a flattering light—how can bookers take them seriously?

There are a number of festival performers who do book themselves, however. Bill Staines still maintains all of his own booking chores. A very popular touring act, the Waybacks, takes care of its own festival schedule. Carol Harley is a member of the group Misty River, but handles the details of their engagements at places like the Winfield, Kansas, festival (a very large five-day event), the Strawberry Festival in Northern California (another large, prestigious festival), and the Sisters Folk Festival in Oregon. Carol is persistent but professional.

All of the band members or individuals booking these acts have things in common: they are relentless self-promoters (and I mean that in the kindest sense possible), they follow up on initial contacts regularly and promptly, and they try to fit into what the festival needs. If the answer is "no" for this year, they are immediately working on making sure they are on the director's radar for next year's program.

The pay you will receive for festivals is commensurate with what the director thinks you are worth and with what they have in their budget to pay you. In a festival that he has not performed at before, someone like Harry Manx might receive $1500 for two or three sets of music. At the Vancouver or Winnipeg, Canada, Folk Festivals, where he has an established reputation as a festival performer and national airplay, he might receive double or three times that amount. Tom Paxton's asking price for flying across the United States to do a festival on the West Coast is $5000. In almost all cases, the festivals provide hotel accommodations and sometimes travel expenses.

Conversely, if you already have a well-paying festival date booked and another opportunity presents itself en route, you can afford to play that gig for a reduced rate to make your travel (particularly if you are driving) more productive. Most festivals, however, have a clause that limits the proximity and dates you can perform that might conflict with their event (for example, a clause that specifies you cannot play with a 100-mile radius of their festival for one week before or one week after).

Agents and managers talk among themselves constantly about fees their artists receive for festivals, trying to get a handle on what they should ask or accept (even though exaggeration among thieves is the rule here). If you are booking yourself independently, you need to talk to others who are doing what you do and try to get a handle on what those numbers are.

CD sales at festivals can be extraordinary, as you are reaching an audience that may be totally unfamiliar with you. Most festivals insist that you sell your CDs through the festival store to help raise money for the festival, and to use volunteers to effect these sales. The festival will generally retain about 10 to 15 percent of your sales for selling them for you.

Eliza Gilkyson has had great success with maximizing her festival profits by doing this.

> The CD sales double my income. When I go out, if I have a show that pays, say, $1500, then I double my gross. Part of the reason for that is I carry my full catalog of CDs. People are just discovering me, so I carry product that I owned before my Red House recordings, I carry at least five or six titles with me. I think anyone who tours knows this, that the more catalog you carry, the better your sales are.
>
> It's a hassle carrying them and shipping them but it is worth it.
>
> So I pretty much double my income but then I have to pay the record company for my copies when I get home, so that cuts it in half again. [Essentially, artists buy CDs from the record company at $6 to $7 per copy. The record companies generally allow the artist to pay them back for these copies after they complete a tour. The difference between the price they pay to the record label and the retail price is the artist's profit.]

When you have CDs you actually own [as opposed to CDs put out by a record label], that is real profit.

Festival Competitions

There is one other way to break into performing at festivals, and this is by entering a "songwriting competition." One of the first of these kinds of competitions took place at the Newport Folk Festival in the 1960s, organized by Peter Yarrow (of the popular group Peter, Paul, and Mary). When the Kerrville Folk Festival was established in 1972, the Newfolk songwriter's competition became a signature event of that Texas gathering. Some of the winners of Kerrville Folk Festival's Newfolk competition have risen to illustrious careers as songwriters and performers, including Nanci Griffith, Lyle Lovett, Lucinda Williams, and many others. This has given the Kerrville competition great notoriety around the world, and they receive more than 1000 entries a year from songwriters who want to become finalists in their competition.

Of the 1000-plus entries, forty finalists are chosen who pay their own expenses to Kerrville, camp at the festival, and have a chance to play their songs on the main stage in an afternoon show. Three winners are selected from those forty finalists, with the first-place songwriter invited to do a short set on the evening main stage.

The Kerrville Folk Festival stresses that everybody who is selected to be a finalist is already a "winner," and careers have indeed been greatly furthered by the competition. If nothing else, just the networking you get to do with fellow musicians and the songs you trade around the ubiquitous all-night campfires are worth the trip. If you are serious about your songwriting/performing career, the Kerrville Folk Festival experience, and the Newfolk song competition in particular, is an important rite of passage that will somehow be beneficial to your career. The Kerrville Folk Festival runs for eighteen days each year, but the songwriting competition always takes place on Saturday of Memorial Day weekend.

By the way, songwriters in other styles of music other than folk (though there is great debate still about what that genre really is) should not be put off by the name. Almost all styles of lyric and melody writing are represented in the Kerrville Newfolk contest.

There are numerous other festivals that also incorporate a songwriting competition into their program. Some, but by no means all, of these festivals are the Sisters (Oregon) Folk Festival, the Falcon Ridge (Connecticut) Folk Festival, and the Telluride (Colorado) Bluegrass Festival. These festivals all include short main-stage sets for the winners of their competitions, and offer other incentives to compete as well.

In 1997 I performed at the Napa Valley Folk Festival in California, and also recorded the songwriting competition there for broadcast on my *River City Folk* radio program. While recording and listening to the musicians involved in the presentation, I heard an extraordinary act by a duo, Dave Carter and Tracy Grammer. Dave Carter was the writer of the songs, and he and his partner rendered the songs with a traditional flair, yet with a very modern and catchy song structure that set them apart from the other entrants that October day. Dave played both banjo and guitar very well, and Tracy switched off between her fiddle, mandolin, and guitar. They both sang very well, and were one of the three winners at the festival that year.

Dave and Tracy followed the songwriting contests across North America, winning a goodly number of them, doing radio dates wherever they could, and scraping by on a few subsistence gigs. Following this course of developing their career, they eventually landed a recording contract with Signature Sounds records in Northampton, Massachusetts, landed a spot as the opening act on a concert tour for Joan Baez (who became a great fan of Dave's songs), and became perhaps the best-known new duo in acoustic music in the early 2000s. They traveled by car, packing all of their instruments and CDs into a Dodge Caravan and driving all the way across the country from the West Coast, with lots of stops in between.

Dave and Tracy are certainly the most successful of all of the artists that I have known who followed the strategy of entering song competitions wherever they could, and becoming known in that fashion. Dave's songs are exceptional mixes of poetry and melody, but it was their commitment to taking a risk and traveling coast to coast, for no guaranteed reward, that made them an act that was a major draw at festivals such as Falcon Ridge. Dave Carter died very suddenly in 2002; Tracy Grammer carries out his legacy, performing his songs in concerts, clubs, and festivals throughout the United States. Her 2005 release, *Flower of Avalon* on Signature Sounds, was the most played CD on acoustic music radio stations that year.

After Dave and Tracy had established themselves on the songwriting competition circuit, they divided the band chores in a way that maximized their strengths. Dave would sit and write and work on songs on a daily basis, and Tracy would do all the business tasks: making booking calls, sending out promotional material and contracts, and charting their tour schedule. They would reunite to work on new Dave Carter songs, and were very meticulous in their arrangements of those compositions. Their stage show incorporated Dave's droll Oklahoma sense of humor but had a sense of the mystical about it as well.

The Jim Fleming Agency took over Dave and Tracy's booking shortly before Dave died, and continues to book Tracy today. Dave and Tracy's organization, musical determination, and commitment to finding a way to support themselves through their music are a great example to musicians trying to accomplish the same goals.

There are other songwriting competitions for the aspiring songwriter aside from the festival events, such as the John Lennon Songwriting Competition and the USA Songwriting Competition. Every songwriting contest, in a festival setting or not, has its own set of politics. Competitions such as the two I listed above, however, are less about the song than they are about eventual commercial revenues for a record company or sponsor. Still, enter your songs in as many competitions as you can bear. Many of them do provide critiques that can be useful. Do not become too discouraged, however, by negative critiques you may get.

The USA Songwriting Competition has been going on for more than ten years now, and offers prizes including radio airplay and a top prize of $50,000. They offer the chance to enter in a number of different categories. You can get an entry form and details at http://www.songwriting.net/entryform.html.

If you enter a songwriting contest, I strongly suggest that you make sure that any demonstration recordings that you submit to the contest contain really good vocal and instrumental performances. Although all of the contests insist that the judges have golden ears and don't need to hear highly "produced" demos, put yourself in their shoes. If you had to listen to a few hundred demos in a day or two, would you tend to pay more attention to the ones that were musically attractive, or recordings that were unpleasant to listen to? It isn't necessary to go overboard and use a fully orchestrated track, but at least be sure that the singing is in tune and attractive, and that the listener can easily understand the lyrics. Once again, common sense needs to come into play. There are many people working in the music business who cannot "hear" a song as being a rock song, for example, unless there are drums on the accompanying track.

Other Considerations about Contests

Before you make a commitment to enter a songwriting contest, there are a number of things to consider. Below is a laundry list of some of these concerns.

Do you understand what prizes you are competing for? For example, some of these contests promise recording time or a record release. Do you have a choice of the studio you will be recording in? How many hours will you receive if you win? Are the hours long enough to enable you to come up with a competitive product? If there is going to be a record release, what is the label, and will there be any promotion of the release? My friend Dick Weissman had an acquaintance who won a $50,000 prize in a national contest and a record release on a major label. When the winner arrived in Nashville to meet his producer, the record executive explained that he had a plane to catch, and gave the "winner" a big ten minutes of his time. When the record was completed, the label honored its commitment to release it, but gave it absolutely no promotion. The singer/songwriter then spent a good chunk of his $50,000 winnings in a fruitless attempt to promote the record. He had no idea that a major label promotion costs far more than that.

If the prize is musical equipment, is it something you really want or need? Remember that if you sell the equipment off, it's going to net you a whole lot less money than the retail selling price of the goods.

Do you have any notion of who you are competing against, and who is judging the songs? If there are, for example, ten thousand entries for a single prize, is this a good use of your time, effort, and money?

Is there an entry fee, and is it a fair amount of money? If the entry fee is $25, and you enter ten songs, you will have spent $250.

How much is it going to cost you to produce a competitive recording of your song? This question involves such matters as whether you have your own home studio, and whether you are going to need to hire other musicians and singers. We have already pointed out that although the contests may imply that the judges can "hear" whether the song is good enough whether or not you submit a well-produced song, this is probably not a realistic assessment of the real situation with tired judges and multiple entries.

THE SONGWRITING PROCESS, CONTINUED: EDITING YOUR SONGS AND EXPANDING YOUR SONGWRITING SUBJECTS AND HORIZONS

The Songwriting Process: Editing

The late Dave Carter was an expert at editing his work. He never shied away from multisyllabic words or poetic license, but he was also able to convey a complete, concise thought and mood in his compositions, which is probably why he won so many songwriting competitions.

For me, each song is a different little odyssey. Some songs seem to immediately transfer to the paper, and I am only the conduit. Others take time to consider and do research on. I write many songs based on history or geography, so often I like to subject the initial draft to a little closer criticism to make sure I am being accurate. My song "Trial by Fire" is a tribute to wilderness firefighters, inspired primarily by being just a few miles from the tragic Storm King Mountain fire in Colorado in 1994, which claimed the lives of fourteen young men and women.

That song was also influenced by Norman Maclean's evocative book *Young Men and Fire,* about a similar fire in 1949 in Montana. I kept the newspaper articles for three years and read the book, until I finally figured out the approach I would take to the song. I eventually wrote six verses and pared them to a concise, storytelling four. It remains one of my most popular songs with audiences around the country.

That fire and the literature on it was a powerful enough event that it caught another songwriter's notice. James Keelaghan from

Calgary, Alberta, wrote a song about the 1949 Montana fire and the foreman of the crew who survived, in another well-known song, "Cold Missouri Waters."

The songs are about basically the same events, but the lyrical focus is very different. I think the contrast in the two songs is a good example of how even narrational song stylings differ from writer to writer.

Harry Manx and Eliza Gilkyson both take a similar tack to the way they write and later edit a song. Harry Manx writes many of his songs on the road, because of his extensive traveling schedule:

> I'm sort of like the guy who makes the maple syrup. I start it out with a hundred gallons and get it down to half a gallon. I write like that. I constantly edit, even during the recording process, if the words aren't working for me properly. Even after I've recorded the album sometimes I sing different words, because I'm still in process of changing them.
>
> It's a funny thing about writing songs, then recording them. I write songs for an album, then quite often I learn to really play them a year or two later, after I have them on the road for a while and I really get into the song.
>
> I think putting a song down on a recording is a snapshot of a moment. It may not be your ultimate or best moment, but after that you have to live with it.

Eliza Gilkyson tries not to limit her creative vision when she is in the early stages of a song. It is a method I have heard many songwriters prescribe to break through to the inspirational discovery phase of writing the song.

> I don't think about editing until I get the big piece together. I don't try to edit early, I think it is dangerous, and you want to let the creative force have its way with you. So I wait, till I have all the elements out there, and then I go back later.
>
> Sometimes when I go back and begin editing I might even eliminate the initial idea that started the song. I will pick a subtler, supporting element and use that as the focus, because it is not as obvious.

Gordon Lightfoot has written many hundreds of songs in his lifetime, and recorded more than 200 of them himself on studio albums. When I asked him about his use of the editing process, his answer was a little different from Harry's or Eliza's response:

I didn't do very much editing. You're talking about the format. I usually would make damn good and sure I had the format before I would even go into the studio with the song.

There is a method that works for me. If I feel I really need to do it, I know how to go about it. But whether or not it's going to have that "magical" quality, as Dylan described on his *60 Minutes* interview, I don't know if that would be there. I can construct them, I can craft them and get it done—but I just don't know if they have that same magical quality as earlier. That's one of those things that make me wonder. I'm going through a stack of them right now. There are about ten songs sitting here, and I'm just not 100 percent positive whether they really hold water or not.

Still, few songwriters have written either the volume or the quality of songs that Lightfoot has crafted over this past almost half century, and his determination to continue to be creative should be an inspiration to all performing singer/songwriters.

Though commercial radio and popular culture focus almost entirely on the theme of boy–girl romance, there are as many topics to write about as there are new people to meet and experiences to have. As I mentioned, I enjoy writing songs about history and geography, as well as more traditional song material. As I began to do this, I was surprised to discover that museums and historical societies began to be interested in my performances, and eventually those kinds of gigs represented a good part of my income. I didn't write those sorts of songs with that intention, but getting a little bit off of the beaten path as a songwriter can be a very wise move.

Gordon Lightfoot had what has to be one of the most unusual songs ever to make it into the U.S. Top Ten with "The Wreck of the Edmund Fitzgerald." Written about the sinking of a Great Lakes iron ore ship that sank in a bad storm in November 1975, the song is constructed in a traditional folk ballad structure, with a detailed narrative, no bridge section, and no chorus. He wrote it after reading a *Newsweek* article about the event. He was very knowledgeable about how the weather can be dangerous in the Great Lakes, having been out in boats in those waters since he was a young boy in Orillia, Ontario.

No one was more surprised than Lightfoot when "The Wreck of the Edmund Fitzgerald" rose to #2 on the U.S. pop charts in 1976. He wrote the song as a tribute to the men who died and to the power of nature, rather than as a commercial song.

Today, it remains in his set list at every concert and he considers that piece one of his proudest songwriting achievements.

I believe it remains a popular song because of the almost mantra quality of the melody, and the well-crafted narrative. Whatever the appeal, it certainly wasn't written with the standard hit formula of the 1970s in mind.

In addition to her heartfelt, intelligent ballads, Eliza Gilkyson has made a name for herself writing a type of song few people even attempt in these times: the political commentary song. I have always been fascinated by artists who are successful at combining their political beliefs with songwriting skills, and I asked her how she goes about doing that.

If you look through my body of work, you will find I was not as political as I am now, but I was always influenced and discouraged by the basic human condition.

What has influenced me and inspired me is being a student of that condition. It has brought me joy and sorrow for my whole songwriting career. It brought me to philosophy and seeking a personal kind of values that would work for me.

I became political myself in a more concrete way with this last invasion into Iraq. I was coming up on it; you can see the evolution starting in the early Red House recordings. I wrote "Riverside," and that was the bridge where I actually crossed my fascination with the human condition with the practicalities of politics. I was making a statement about this hopeless repeating of patterns that human beings seem to do, with war and self-destruction and patriarchy. So I crossed that bridge over into current times: "We sleep so easily, burn the oil like it's free, watch the war on TV, with God on our side."

I do not encourage people to write political or message music. Most times I can't stand it, and I hate to be preached at. I think it is much better to craft a great song than a political song. If someone is going to do one or the other, I would rather they gave me a great piece of music, a well-crafted song, rather than something that is boring.

On the other hand, if the political song is a natural progression, and it is musical, it can be powerful. This is one of the things that Phil Ochs did so well, and it was fun listening to his music. He had great pop melodies, and wonderful guitar hook lines. He was just a great songwriter, who happened be affected by politics. It was natural for him to do that, and the same with Dylan. It was searing poetry, no matter what the subject was. That's what got me, about either of those guys.

"Tender Mercies" is my favorite song that I have written about politics. Once again, it is where the human condition meets activism. The solution, if there is one, for the current corner that we have painted ourselves into, is we must find what we have in common ... even with our enemies.

That was the point of that song, that even the mother of a suicide bomber wants the same thing for her child that a mother in this country wants. You want your child to be safe and to grow up with certain comforts. I think every mother wants the same thing. They want their children to live long, fruitful, blessed lives.

Any child that is in a situation that they are willing to strap a bomb to their chest ... something is so wrong in that world, that their quality of life is such they don't care for their life or others' lives.

What I am trying to do in that song is bridge that gap between us and our enemies.

That song angers people, too. People think that the song is about supporting suicide bombing, which it is not. It is about somewhere out there, a mother has lost a child.

What I want to do with songs like that, and songs like "Requiem," is create an emotional connection with others in this world who are suffering. I think it is important for us in this affluent country to realize that with every bit of comfort that we have, there are people around the world who have less because of our comfort. I don't think people want to make that painful connection. They want to think there is enough for everyone in the world, and there is not.

Eliza has become an established concert draw not only for her musical abilities but also because she has the courage to write about what she believes in and because she presents it in a listenable and compelling form. By working and writing well outside of the parameters of popular culture, she has created her own successful career that not only entertains people but also makes them examine their own beliefs.

Harry Manx, while not writing music that is overtly political, transcends songwriting boundaries in his own way as he composes his cross-cultural compositions.

I was interested in Eastern spiritualism and meditation specifically, and I sat with quite a few masters in India the twelve years I was there. I started to become a meditator and to think about life in a different way, what is and what isn't important to me. Love plays a big role in my life, and needs to play a larger role. Because that is my perspective on myself, that is also what is reflected in the songs. Love, life, death, and laughter—subjects like this, they are not to be taken too lightly. Those are very intense experiences for all of us, and I try to write about those kinds of things.

RECORDING AND DISTRIBUTING YOUR OWN ALBUM OR SIGNING WITH AN ESTABLISHED COMPANY?

If you are recording your own album, there are various ways of distributing it. They include:

- Selling it at your shows.
- Consigning it to record stores.
- Contacting a digital distributor, such as CD Baby, to sell it on the Internet (we cover this in more detail at the end of Chapter 7).
- Finding a regional or national independent distributor. These companies stock product from hundreds of labels. They are not apt to invest in promoting your product, but they can assist you in deciding how to spend what promotional dollars you have to invest.
- Distributing through a major label. This is a rare occurrence; to make it happen, you need to have major regional sales in order to interest a major label.
- Sending the album out to newspaper and magazine critics, especially in publications that specialize in the genre of music that you work in.

Another way to promote your album is to hire an independent promoter who specializes in obtaining airplay for independent artists. The more markets that you want them to cover, the more you will have to pay them. You will need to set aside a number of albums for promotional giveaways, and you will need to determine how many weeks you want to continue promoting the album.

While the number of album releases has increased exponentially, the number of successful major and independent record labels certainly has not. The major record label consolidation that began in the late 1960s has continued to the point where there are really fewer than half a dozen major record labels, with many subsidiaries.

Some good news is that smaller independent labels continue to survive and bring new music to the forefront. Saddle Creek Records in Omaha, Nebraska, has grown to a point of enviable profitability by bringing the songs of Conor Oberst and groups like Feint to a young national audience. Oberst shared stages with artists like Bruce Springsteen during the 2004 presidential campaign, and sells out shows in medium-sized halls all across the United States.

Another Omaha, Nebraska, company, American Gramaphone Records, is a label that primarily records and distributes the music of its founder, Chip Davis. Each of its albums of Christmas music by Mannheim Steamroller, Chip's group, has gone platinum (certified sales of more than 1 million units). From the initial seed money Chip earned from writing the music to the hit 1970s song "Convoy," he has created an empire that sells not only records but also other related lifestyle products as well.

Harry Manx, like Chip Davis, is the president/owner of his own record label, and thus has all of his music under his own control, which is definitely a plus if you can figure out how to effectively do that.

> I think the only minus could be if you try to do it all yourself. I have hired a couple of people to run the record business for me, because I saw there was a lot more work in it than I could give the time to.
>
> The pluses are many. You go from making 10 percent with a label to making 90 percent from your albums. I still think it is a good thing to sign with a label for an artist who is just emerging, because that label is going to spend some money promoting you and building your reputation in the retail market, and that is very important.
>
> If you are an independent artist, it is probably good to have someone put up money to promote you properly in the beginning. Once you are known, which is what happened to me after three albums, then I could do my own record company. But still, you need to get good distribution for your record company. Without proper distribution you are in the same zone again, of having 100 percent of nothing.
>
> We are situated well now. We are distributed well, and the albums sell well. But it was a little scary going out there on my own. I was wondering if I was ever going to sell another record after I quit that last label I was with.

Harry has been very successful recording, marketing, and distributing his own albums, and is now looking to build his label with other original artists who also are highly original and motivated. His album income has grown to be a significant percentage of his total.

The touring makes up about 60 percent, and the rest is from selling CDs. But the profits from the selling of that product, I tend to plow everything that comes in back into the company, to try to make my next record, to pay for other artists we want to promote, and such things. I think of it as an investment in my future to build a label that will take care of me after I stop taking care of it.

That's what I am doing at the moment, and I am sort of gambling on the fact that we will be able to find enough good artists to make the label successful down the road.

However, in the current record sales market, these independent label success stories are few and far between.

As discussed in Chapter 4, when an artist signs with a label, the label gives the artist an advance to do the album. Those costs are paid back to the label from record royalties. The label will also front the artist promotional costs, which for a major label can be as much as half a million dollars or more. Again, these costs will be taken out of artist royalties.

Of course, a record label will generally take care of distribution of your album, getting it into the stores, and you will have a much higher profile publicly with an established label than if you produce your own album and sell it yourself.

Some small record labels, such as Waterbug in Chicago, are run essentially as artist co-ops. The artist pays for the cost of his or her own album. Waterbug handles some of the distribution for the album, and includes it in their catalog, for a small percentage of total sales.

More often on small labels, the artist is advanced the anticipated cost of the CD, and the artist will pay back that cost out of future royalties. The label sends out 400 to 600 promotional copies of the CD to radio stations and publications for review, and does whatever other promotion for the release is agreed upon. The artist buys his or her sales copies from the label at $6 to $8 a copy, and resells them in live performances for $15 or so. The record company distributes the album to retail stores.

People who should know have told me that less than 10 percent of all CD releases in the United States ever sell 1000 copies or more (I have no idea how they got that number, but it sounds about right). Also, the vast majority of sales for smaller artists happen at live performances, rather than at record stores.

With all of these factors in mind, and from what you know about how much an album should cost you, why sign with a label at all unless you are the new Beck or Toby Keith? This is a question all songwriters have to answer for themselves, taking into account their individual aspirations and ambitions. Try to be as objective as you can if you have to make this decision, about your talent, songs, and willingness to give up a "normal" life for total dedication to promoting yourself and your music.

For songwriter/performers who want to tour extensively, having the kind of distribution a record label will provide is very important. If you do not have that label, it is natural to try to obtain record store distribution on your own. However, Terry Currier, of Burnside Distribution in Portland, Oregon, has a question that all artists trying to expand their audiences should ask themselves:

> The first question should be, does the artist really need distribution? Distribution can get your product out to a certain amount of stores, based on what the artist demand is in the marketplace. If there isn't a demand in the marketplace, distribution doesn't need to be made.
>
> Artists think that they need to get distribution right away, especially if they're working within a region of the country.
>
> In 1986, it was known as "regional distribution," and there were about six of those in the U.S. that distributed for Untied Artists, Rounder, whoever. Any independent label that was around in 1986, that is the way it worked, and you made a deal with them.
>
> Then, one day, Tower Records made a decision: "Why are we buying this label from six different distributors and paying six different prices, and processing six different invoices, when we should only be doing it with one?"
>
> So Tower mandated that they would only buy from one distributor. So all of the regional distributors scrambled to become national distributors, because that was the only way they were going to stay in business.
>
> When there was regional distribution, things were more customer based than when that distributor had to take care of the whole country. So there was a lot of disconnect when we went to national distribution, and a lot fewer distributors knew what their customer base needed.
>
> When there was regional distribution, it was the best deal for the new artists. They could just go up to a Seattle-based distributor, and work that market and build a sales base, beginning with that region.
>
> But now if that artist goes to the same distributor who works nationally, why is someone in Boston going to buy that album, or someone in Nebraska going to buy that album? There has to

be some reason for the retailer to buy that album. Do you have a weekly syndicated radio show? Are you going to be getting reviews in national magazines? Are you going on a national tour opening for an established act?

If there's not a compelling reason for that national distribution, then artists should build their own networks by going to record stores, putting records in on consignment, and building their careers to a point where they really do need distribution.

You'll know when you are at that level when you are bringing the records into stores yourself and you can't keep up with the demand of filling up the bins.

Eliza Gilkyson's label, Red House Records out of Minneapolis, Minnesota, has consistently done well with her albums, but she regrets never having had the chance to present her music to an even larger audience:

I've had no major-label experience. I've always been outside that realm, and in the past, it was heartbreaking to me. It made me have to work a lot harder. The one difference with the major labels is they have a publicity machine that small labels can't compete with.

With a small label you have creative control, you get a lot of attention, and personal relationships with independent labels that you wouldn't have with a major label. But, there is absolutely no way you can break a record into the mainstream market without the $250,000 to $500,000 that is required, that the major labels provide. There are no exceptions to that.

You have to *pay* now for shelf space in the record stores. It's not a passive thing. You pay for radio time, you pay for advertising, you pay for your shelf space; there's that sum you have to ante up just to play the game.

I am just happy there is another world out there that I can survive in.

THE IMPORTANCE OF PRODUCERS IN THE RECORDING PROCESS

Having a producer in the studio first and foremost gives you another set of ears to evaluate objectively what is being recorded. As a singer, it allows you to concentrate on your interpretation of your song, knowing that you have an advocate who will honestly tell you if the piece needs to be sung again, if your guitar is out of tune, or if the arrangement just doesn't work.

However, that is just a small part of what most record producers do. A producer will work with you on the arrangement of your song(s), suggesting musical hooks and writing parts for the instruments you want to feature on a particular composition. Producers often have ties with publishers and other music business types who can be a great help to a songwriter's career.

A producer can be a fellow musician whom you recruit to help in the recording process, or it can be someone such as David Foster, who will be paid $50,000 to $100,000 plus a percentage of the profits, and oversee virtually every part of the process.

Gordon Lightfoot has had a number of different producers throughout his long career. Most of the hit albums in the 1970s were made with Warner Brothers producer Lenny Waronker, but he has also worked with John Simon, David Foster, and produced a few of them himself.

> I always worked well with my producers … we were a team. At Warner/Reprise, I worked with the same guy on about eight albums. We really got to know each other, and the kind of results we wanted to get. I learned a lot.
>
> The producers at that time always let me be a full partner in the mix. I had a great engineer at Warner/Reprise too, Lee Hershberg.
>
> As that was taking place, knowing that I was capable of doing the basic tracks, they would let me do those tracks here [in Toronto]. Then they would come up, and as things went along, they would let me do the whole thing here, then go down to L.A. and let Lenny [Waronker] and I decide what else to put on it. But I would do the basic tracks here. Then, I just started doing the whole thing when it came down towards the end of the record contract with them.
>
> It didn't matter by that time anyway, because they were no longer behind me by the time I got to albums 13 and 14. I was just finishing the contract, and the push was off. I was determined to finish the contract anyway, so I went ahead and did so.
>
> I'm still going, and I don't want to stop. There's a whole bunch of other people around me who don't want to stop, either. We'll be among those who bop until they drop.

I have had the opportunity to produce a few other folks' albums through the years, such as Wyoming songwriter Chris Kennedy and Chicago performer Marty Peiffer. It is a very demanding position and you feel responsible for making the best album possible for the artist. Cowriter Dick Weissmam has also worked as a producer on many record projects.

The artist/producer relationship is crucial if the album is to succeed. I have used the same producer on my past five albums—Clete Baker of Omaha, Nebraska. Clete is knowledgeable, opinionated, and musically very astute. He is also relentlessly positive, though he will always tell me when he feels something is not quite right or he feels I can do a better job with another pass at it. We don't always agree, but I trust his judgment.

Eliza Gilkyson talks about why she uses a producer, and how important he is to her creative process in the studio.

> There are times when I just want to be an artist... . I don't want to think technically, I just want to create. The time where I most need my producer is when I am doing the basic tracks. I can really lose it there. I can't tell what something sounds like. I'm just sitting there with my guitar and singing, and I just don't have the overview. Later on, I'm good at the process, and Mark turns a lot of the overdub choices over to me. But I have to say, over fifteen or sixteen years with the same producer, there is a lot of trust there. I can turn a lot of choices over to him. We are a team, and I have no interest in doing an album without him.
>
> I'm always surprised that people switch producers so often. It takes years to develop that trust ... it's like changing partners. I know that some folks just want somebody else's vision of their work, but I have such a hard time imagining how you build trust with that new producer.

Producer fees are as variable as the income levels of the performers making the albums. If you are just starting out as a recording songwriter, at least find someone who can evaluate your vocal performance and tell you whether you are in tune with yourself and with whatever other instruments are on the track. You'll be glad you have the help.

As you move along in your career, many artists such as Eliza Gilkyson and Harry Manx will dedicate one quarter of their total album budget to the producer's fees for any given project.

Harry Manx's producer works with him as a confidante, assists with business decisions, and actually records Harry's very successful records in his house:

> I prefer to record close to home. I live on Saltspring Island, British Columbia, and my producer lives just a stone's throw away. So we usually just hire a recording engineer from Victoria. Because of

the state of the art, he can carry the whole studio onto the ferry. He sets up in a good room in my producer's house, and I come over there, and I will play 4 or 5 hours a day for about a week, and get the whole album down.

I don't like to stay a long time in the studio. I find you get jaded after a certain period of time. When I say that, I'm talking about time per day, and also I don't like to spend more than a week. I rehearse extensively until the songs are as good as I can play them, and I just do it.

I take a few runs at the song, and if it is not happening at that point, both my producer and I say, "Maybe leave this song out, and the next album we'll pick it up."

We try to catch a live kind of sound, and if they close their eyes, it sounds as if I am over in the corner playing for them. That is what I would really like the albums to sound like.

I would like it to sound like it does in a live situation. I think that is important.

While Harry Manx is after a live kind of sound and can do an album in a week, recording a pop album for a major label can take a month or even much longer.

One of the most cited examples of this is Fleetwood Mac's Grammy-award-winning hit album *Rumors,* recorded when multitrack over-dubbing was just starting to be used extensively. Not one vocal or instrumental phrase in any song is intact from the original tracks recorded; all of them have many overdubs and edits. This process required months and a massive budget. The album produced many hits and huge sales, but that was the point where many artists and producers began to wonder where musicality stopped and technology took over as the dominant factor in hit records.

7

CREATING AN AUDIENCE FOR YOUR SONGS

THE ROLES OF AGENTS, MANAGERS, AND PUBLICISTS

Booking Agent

Every performing singer/songwriter starts out as his or her own booking agent, learning how to book the gigs and deal with all the associated headaches of making sure you have work six months or a year from now. I currently do all of my own booking, though I have worked through many agents in the past. Bryan Bowers, the virtuosic, charismatic autoharp concert performer, has built a very lucrative and successful career by making his own booking decisions. The popular East Coast–based songwriter Tom Rush used to say to me, "No one cares more about your own bread on your table more than you do," and he booked himself for many years, though he uses an agency now.

When you decide you need an agent to further your career:

- Identify agents who handle music and performers similar to the kind you write and play yourself.
- Attempt to contact these agents by phone and ascertain if they are taking on new artists or are open to hearing new material.
- If the answer is yes, immediately send off a promotional package and recording to them. Do not wait for them to contact you, but follow up with a call two weeks later to see if they received it and had time to review it. When they have reviewed it, even if they have rejected you as a client, ask them for any other ideas they might have about someone who can represent you. Since

they have listened to your presentation and songs, also ask if they have any constructive criticism for you.

- If the answer is "No, I am not taking on new clients," ask them whom they might recommend that you contact to represent you.
- As in so many other aspects of the music business, be sure to consult with your peers about who is representing them and what agents' doors they might be able to open for you.

In my experience, I have found that booking agents tend to make a lot of promises they cannot possibly keep, preying on your reluctance to do the work yourself. They take 15 to 20 percent of your fee for the gig, and you have to provide them with promotional materials and a Web site, and often reimburse their other expenses as well.

On the other hand, Eliza Gilkyson talked earlier in the book about how she feels her career turned the corner when the Val Denn Agency took over her bookings. She attributes much of her success today to her hardworking agent.

It is one of the more thankless jobs there is—trying to sell yourself to a festival, concert venue, or club, and convince the director, promoter, or owner that you are worth what you ask and that you will do the job in a more compelling way than the other performers and agents who are clamoring for the same spot. Learn how to do it yourself and get comfortable with the aggravation of it all. Someday you may be fortunate enough to have a competent agent who takes over your booking for you, but I would not count on it. Until you reach a high level of performance fee, usually around $2000 to $3000 per show, the arithmetic for the agent and you to both make a living just isn't going to pencil out.

Consequently, it is essential that you be able to understand and accomplish every task that you would prefer an agent do for you, no matter how difficult and uncomfortable it may be. Even if you do reach that level, it would serve you well to have a basic understanding and empathy for what your booking agent has to do on a daily basis to keep the gigs coming in.

I wish I could count the number of times a performer has said to me, "I would be a full-time musician if I could only find a good manager or agent who would handle me." This is similar to the old chicken-and-egg dilemma about which comes first. If you have not already figured out how to make yourself somewhat successful by being able to book gigs and handle your own business, the chances that an agent is going to be interested in you are roughly the same as winning the lottery.

Harry Manx sees it this way:

About deals—should we take this deal, that deal—I'll talk to my producer and agency about such things and we will decide what is best. So I don't need any cigar-smoking guy behind a desk taking 20 percent of everything that comes through there.

The booking agency is probably the most important part of your career. If you're not getting any work, the whole thing starts winding down pretty quick. They need to be able to sell you, and to that end you have to help them by putting out a good album regularly, and continuously do good shows to build up your reputation. That way, they only have to pick up the phone and work out the price; they don't have to spend an hour trying to convince the venue that the guy is worth having.

I found such an agency in Canada. In the past few years, they have gone from just having a few artists to having about sixty artists today. Live Tour Artists in Oakville, Ontario [just outside of Toronto], is that agency.

Although the percentage of commissions that an agent gets is usually set at 15 to 20 percent, I have periodically run across local or regional agents who never tell you exactly what percentage they will be taking. Instead, they will call a musician and say, "Alex, I have a client who is interested in having your four-piece band play an engagement at Hotel X. What kind of money do you need to make that happen?" In such a situation, the agent will usually not tell you what the budget for the event is. Let's say that you quote $500 for the gig. The agent then gets back to you, and you sign a contract.

Under those circumstances, I have known an agent to take as much as 50 percent of the proceeds, or even more. If you ever catch the agent doing this, she will justify this outrageous commission by saying, "Alex, I gave you what you asked for." My coauthor, Dick Weissman, once played a gig where the client asked the band leader to take the check so that he wouldn't have to bother mailing it from his out-of-state home. The leader was surprised to discover that the agent had taken 50 percent of the gross!

One good test of an agent's zeal in representing you is the question of whether your fee increases when you replay a club. If the owner has been happy with your act and the club has done good business, then the agent should really try to get you a wage increase. If the agent is more concerned with keeping an account than in representing an act, she might tend not to ask for any additional money, even though she might well be able to get it.

One thing to keep in mind is to be extremely careful before you sign an exclusive agreement with an agent. If you are working in a particular city, it is quite possible to take jobs from more than one agent. If you sign an exclusive agreement, dealing with multiple agents is not permissible. From the artist's side of things, if you do indeed sign with an agent, you should not book work behind his back. The chances are that he can get you enough additional money for a gig to justify his commission, and then some. It is a good idea to be suspicious of any promoter or venue that asks you to go behind an agent's back. It isn't your welfare they have in mind, it's the possibility of saving the money that they would have to pay the agent.

Managers

Managers are another kind of professional assistance that can be useful when you reach a certain income and business level. The booking agent books the gigs; the manager works with them, negotiates your record contract, promotional appearances, helps place you in movies or ads, and advises you on what your next professional move should be. A manager acts as kind of an "executive producer" to your whole career.

Performing singer/songwriters are an independent bunch, and it takes an extraordinary level of trust (and a substantial income, since managers take 20 percent or more of your gross income) to turn over the direction of your total creative output to someone else. Harry Manx is one of the singer/songwriters I know who has tried this, and he says,

> I went through six managers, and I always wound up telling them how my career should be run. I was always bringing them up to date on the vision and direction. So I finally gave up on career managers, and hired a fantastic office manager/secretary. She does everything I need to have done. I will simply point her in the direction of the task—for instance, my itinerary—[and she will] make the calls about car rentals, flights, etc., and it is a full-time job for her.

That is the kind of help that artists really need.

On the other hand, an artist like Gordon Lightfoot, who has his own production company (Early Morning Productions in Toronto, Canada) has numerous aspects of his career that a manger can be a great help for: administering publication royalties, coordinating concert travel, signing contracts with sound companies, negotiating with sidemen, and many other matters that the artist doesn't necessarily want to deal with. Lightfoot talked to me about how grateful he is to his management team that they provide him with the time he needs to write and work on his music. They can wade through the minutiae of such a complicated, successful career and bring him the essential facts about the decisions he needs to make and when he finally needs to make them.

On the positive side, a good manager fulfills a number of roles that an artist will have difficulty doing on his or her own. Although many artists seem to feel that once they have signed a record deal, their careers will skyrocket, a good manager will "work" a record company the way a coach will put together a winning team. The manager should be on a first-name basis with virtually every person in the record company, should fight with the company to get better promotional muscle for your record, will be involved in the cover art and album notes, will try to get the act more advance money, and will make sure that the record company is aware of any gigs that you are playing so that your CDs will be in the local record stores and at radio stations. A sizeable record company has many acts, and your manager will fight to make sure that your act isn't lost in a maze of new releases.

Another positive role of a manager is to know enough about an act to realize its potential in another context. There may be a person in the band who can write film scores, be an actor, or earn additional money as a model. The manager should always have his antennae up to grasp any opportunities that will expand an act's income and get more media attention. Some of the larger management firms are now even involved with record promotion, because as record companies have reduced their staffs and promotional dollars, the manager will attempt to utilize any contacts that he or she has in the industry.

Managers can also be a great help in placing songs with publishing companies or other artists. Certainly the Grossman/Court organization was incredibly successful in getting artists like Bob Dylan and Gordon Lightfoot set up with excellent New York publishers who would place their songs. Of course, the quality of the songs had something to do with that, too!

Sometimes even strong management teams like Lightfoot's have trouble placing music in the extremely competitive, bottom-line-driven music market of today.

We made a really solid attempt to place some material in Nashville about twelve years ago, and didn't have any success there. Perhaps we didn't go about it in the right manner. It's tough; there are a lot of singers and songwriters around Nashville.

I had my moments there, and I had some results there. I made three or four albums down there, enjoyed working there, and always had a great time there. I'd like to work there again sometime. I was supposed to work with Ricky Skaggs, but we never got around to that. He didn't mind working with capoed bands.

I always would take that into consideration. I didn't like going into studios where the studio musicians would have to put capos on their guitars, like we did. They don't mind doing that, but it was still a consideration on my part. Some of them can play in all keys, but some of them can't. A guy like Ricky Skaggs doesn't care about that.

That's what folk music is really … capoed music. Then there is blues, and all the other stuff. But that is the best way I can describe folk music … capoed music.

Capos are a bar across the neck of the guitar that raises the key of the song to suit the singer, without having to use uncomfortable and difficult-to-play voicings of chords. They allow folk and country artists to play finger-style arrangements that would be nearly impossible without the capo, but they can sometimes be a nightmare because of the tuning problems they cause. These are the kinds of artists' problems that no one, not even a great manager, can solve for you!

Publicists

The other member that major artists and record companies rely upon to build an artist's career is the publicist. The publicist coordinates all album promotion, making sure the promo copies of the CD are sent to the target markets and proper individuals. They also have connections to make sure the album gets reviewed in newspapers and magazines.

Depending on the artist, the publicist is generally hired per album project or concert tour. Many artists, even very successful ones, rely upon either their manager or agent to do these tasks, but a publicist can be an important and valuable element to a successful tour, album, or career.

For artists who employ a manager, agent, and publicist, the total costs can easily exceed 50 percent of their gross income.

TOURING: DOMESTIC AND INTERNATIONAL

As a songwriter/performer, if you are going to get your music heard, you are most likely going to have to do some traveling—probably a *lot* of traveling.

Setting up a tour of gigs that pay for themselves is an art unto itself. If you have an agent doing this for you, you are fortunate (if they wind up booking you into places where you will draw a crowd and make a profit). But even if that is the case, you need to be thoroughly acquainted with what is doable and what is not. In other words, having an itinerary that has you driving from Rock Springs, Wyoming, to Coffeyville, Kansas, and then doing a show that same night is going to be awfully tough on you.

Assuming that early in your career (and perhaps all through your performing life) you will be handling the travel agent duties yourself, how do you start to tour regionally, then nationally, then finally overseas?

When you begin to look beyond your performing hometown and base, try to find a club or concert series that features the kind of music that you write and play yourself. Whether this place is 100, 1000, or 3000 miles away, pursue it aggressively as the anchor to your tour in that area. Most of these "anchor" gigs that give you concert exposure and pay far more than your usual asking price at home come about from personal connections. Do you know someone connected with a college or university who might be able to get your foot in the door with the student programming committee there? Do you have friends who will petition a local community concert series to squeeze you in? Is there an old high school acquaintance somehow involved with city government who might have a connection to get you a parks concert? If you really think about questions like these, you are going to find a "yes" answer somewhere, and it is up to you to follow it up.

This summer I am doing a concert at a very prestigious concert series, outdoors, at a very upscale lodge. They only put on four concerts a year. A group of folks who enjoy my music wrote and called requesting they book my trio for a concert, unbeknownst to me. The promoter contacted me, and we struck a deal. Again, often in this business, it is who you know and who believes in you that makes all the difference between a successful tour and career and one that is financially not worthwhile.

Most concert and gig tours will not consist of a winner every night, in every town you perform in. However, it is paramount that you have enough well-paying anchor gigs to pay for your gas, airfare, or rental cars. On some tours your profit margin may only be your CD sales, after expenses. Some tours that take you to a new region may not be profitable at all, but will hopefully build a base for the next time you pass through that area.

You really have to have a fire within to put yourself (and your band, if you have one) through the rigors of performing extensively on the road. In these days of $3 a gallon gas, "cheap" hotels that cost more than $50, and musicians' wages that have not risen appreciably over the years, it is a tough equation to make touring work for you. Still, if you are serious about connecting with people and getting your songs out there, touring is essential.

Even if you are used to having folks perform with you on your songs when you are at home, consider improving your skills to a level that you can perform solo when you are on tour. In most cases, particularly when you are starting out, it is impossible to get a concert/gig tour to pencil out if you have sidemen involved.

Once you have secured the anchor gig for the region—for instance, you have a concert at Creighton University in Omaha that will pay you $1000 on a Saturday night, and you live in Denver—start searching the Internet and networking with other musicians about gigs you might be able to pick up along the way. If there is a place in North Platte that is willing to pay you even $200 on a Tuesday or Wednesday night, that will give you your gas money (one way, these days) from Denver to Omaha. Plus, as I have said so many times in this book, you never know whom you might meet at that North Platte gig. If you are going to make that trip from Denver to Omaha, try to pick up engagements in North Platte, Grand Island, Des Moines, Iowa, and perhaps even Kansas City on the way back. Colleges and universities are always a possibility, and though many of them book through organizations such as NACA, many colleges' Offices of Student Affairs independently arrange a wide variety of shows.

These secondary engagements may not have the glamour and pay of the anchor gig, but they are what will ultimately make a tour profitable.

Touring to play music, doing a variety of gigs and concerts, is just about the most fun you can have in this business when things are going well. In addition to the importance of connecting with a wide cross-section of people who might be able to help you out or will enjoy your music, you need to do it because it is really the frosting on the cake. The sweetest part of all the struggles and aggravation is the full hall, enthusiastic audience, and standing ovation in a town or theater you have not played before.

Plus, of course, the more life and human experience we observe as songwriters, the better our songs are going to be. Traveling while touring to do concerts and gigs is not like traveling as a young executive with a major corporation; you are going to meet all kinds of people, sleep in all kinds of beds, and experience all kinds of highs and lows. For the songwriter who truly wants to write and sing the best songs he or she possibly can, there is no substitute for getting out on the road and putting it all on the line.

There are a number of songwriter/performers whom I have talked to through the years that agree with me upon one point: do not limit yourself to just the largest cities. Oftentimes in larger communities, the entertainment options are so many that even with good publicity and promotion you can have a terrible turnout for one of your gigs. When that happens, no matter the size of the town or the prestige of the venue, you are not helping yourself. You have to have at least a minimal attendance to build upon for the next time you perform in that area.

In smaller communities, people tend to be more appreciative, less guarded, and have more time to visit with you. I have also always found I tend to sell more CDs in smaller towns where the attendance is good than in bigger cities where I might have just as many people in the audience.

For many years, I would spend about six months a year on the road, 500 or more miles away form my home in Omaha, Nebraska. Omaha, while having the advantage of being centrally located in the United States, was not exactly awash in opportunities for songwriter/performers. I established my reputation at that point in my life by spending the fall traveling to the West Coast and to Alaska, and in the springtime I would head east, to Boston, Virginia, the Carolinas, and points in between. In between, I would fly to select festivals and concerts when it made financial or professional sense to do so.

Still, I had opportunities in the mid-size city of Omaha that I never would have had in, say, Boston (where I lived and performed in 1977 to 1978). I started my national radio broadcast *River City Folk* there, was enlisted to tape thirty-two episodes of a national cable television program, and eventually wound up doing a series of concerts with the Omaha Symphony Orchestra accompanying me on my songs.

Having a symphony orchestra play complete arrangements of my songs with me on stage remains one of the highlights of my career. Bruce Hangen, the musical director and conductor of the Omaha Symphony Orchestra in the early 1990s, had seen me perform when I was home in Omaha many times at a small club, with my trio occasionally joining me. He listened to my radio program regularly, and even more importantly, knew that I traveled and performed nationally.

Rhoda McIntire, the manager of the Omaha Symphony, suggested I drop off a CD of my most recent album at the office for Hangen to hear. I did so, and also enclosed a promotional package, never thinking it would actually lead to a gig.

I was on the road in South Carolina preparing to do a concert when Bruce Hangen called me and asked me to headline a symphony program the next year. I was excited and amazed. I did a series of three concerts with full orchestral arrangements to many of my songs, in front of a pops symphony audience of 2500 people each night.

Despite all of that, I still had to hit the road early and often to stay busy. With my westerner's mentality, I always considered anything within 500 miles to be a "local" trip (meaning I could make it home after the concert if I really needed to, since it was only a 7- or 8-hour drive).

Using that parameter as a yardstick, if you don't have enough gigs where you are and want to get out of town, try your luck in some exotic clime like Baggs, Wyoming, or Mt. Pleasant, Iowa.

Look at an atlas. Establish a 500-mile radius from where you are. If you know any reputable concert venues within that radius, what are you waiting for? Call them, send them promotional packages, make sure they know you are ready to play for them next week, next month, or next year. The first phone call or promo package probably won't do the trick, but be persistent. Offer to do an opening act, or even make the drive to play at an open mike the venue sponsors, if the owner/booker says he will be there and will listen to your songs.

There are a number of gig touring guides that have sprung up in recent years, put out by individuals and organizations like the Kerrville Folk Festival. I have had a pretty constant circuit of festivals and gigs in recent years, so I can't really recommend a particular one, but you should choose one to purchase and glean every bit of information it has to offer.

When you put together a tour of a few gigs to a new area for the first time, don't be discouraged if you only break even on the trip, after expenses. This is a very common experience when a songwriter/performer is attempting to break into a new area.

Though it is not the most comfortable way to travel, when you are starting out touring, always try to avail yourself of free accommodations. Many clubs owners will offer you a place to stay, usually in their house, if you ask them for lodgings. Universities and colleges often have dorm rooms available, if you do not have a motel room in your contract and it is out of your budget.

Hopefully you are not allergic to cats or dogs and you are not terribly averse to sleeping in your car or camping, if need be. These are part of the realities of touring, too, when you are starting out.

There is a famous story by Bill Staines, which he frequently has told me, about one of his first trips to Alaska. The promoter picked him up at the airport, and Staines inquired as to whether there had been many calls about the concert. The promoter said, "No, not too many." Staines then asked if there seemed to be a lot of interest in his music, which had been played on the Juneau public radio station. To that question, the promoter said, "Well, not really." Staines's third and final question to the fellow asked if he thought there would be many people at the concert that night. The promoter replied, in an understated way, "I wouldn't count on it."

Well, there were not too many people in the show in Juneau that night, but Staines persisted through the years, and built a very strong base of support for himself and his songs throughout Alaska. He has a fine book about his life traveling to play music called *The Road: A Life between the Lines,* published by Xlibris Press.

For Americans performing in Canada, you will need to get a letter from a nonprofit organization certifying that you are doing a benefit concert for them, if you want to legally enter Canada with yourself and your guitar. Even with that letter, you will be charged $150 for a work permit. If you are playing at a Canadian folk festival or major venue, they will take care of the paperwork for you. Otherwise, you are on your own. I lived and performed in Canada for years, and crossed the border numerous times, sometimes with the legal papers, sometimes with a tall tale straight out of Chaucer. It was not so hard to do back in those days; in these times, with the computer processing at the border and increased security, you would be well advised to have all of your paperwork in order.

For Canadians trying to perform in the United States, the process is even more rigorous. You have to apply months in advance for your work visa, showing that the music that you do is unique artistically. Your employers or promoters have to fill out and sign affidavits with your application that verify your concert dates, and cultural worth. The whole experience of playing shows in the United States is difficult, and as a Canadian you will have to be organized and determined to make it happen.

While having an agent is not absolutely essential if you are booking a concert in North America, it will serve you well to find someone who will book you into the concerts, clubs, and festivals if you are traveling overseas and hope to make it pay.

Search the Internet for agents, network with fellow musicians, or consult a good trade magazine such as *MOJO* magazine, out of the United Kingdom, or *Folk Roots* magazine, also from the United Kingdom. You will see listings in there for both agents and clubs overseas.

However, just as when you set up a tour over here to a new region, the most effective way to start is with a personal connection somewhere in the area who can make some face-to-face contacts for you.

DEALING WITH THE DREADED "WRITER'S BLOCK"

There is nothing more discouraging to the serious performing singer/songwriter than those stretches of time when the inspiration just doesn't come, and the songs just are not flowing like they once did. Every composer experiences these times, and it is important as artists that we learn some of the techniques other writers use to get started writing again.

Chuck Pyle, the prolific and talented Colorado songwriter, once told me that when his imagination fails him, he learns a song by someone else that he has been meaning to play. He says that by doing this, his own thought processes start moving again.

There are schools and books that talk at length about methods to write songs, and they suggest writing something every day, keeping a pad of paper and pen by your bed and in your car, and so on.

However, there doesn't seem to be a lot written about those times when your brain is just tired from the creative process. Even someone who has seemed to have his method down and who has written hundreds of songs has these periods. When I went backstage to see Gordon Lightfoot in 1988, I was shocked to hear he hadn't written any songs in a couple of years, and didn't know if he would ever write any again. It was finally the motivation to finish his recording commitments that got him writing again, and he hasn't stopped since. At the time, though, he said he was considering "retiring" from songwriting.

> How long ago was that? The late eighties? Jeez, I guess I was wrong about that. I had two more albums to go for Warner Brothers, and I really wanted to finish that contract. People were leaving, and I knew it was time for me to go too, and I figured I'd better get those last two albums done.
>
> After I finished those, the songs for my twentieth studio album, *Harmony*, were written with no particular record label in mind. The resulting album came out on Linus Entertainment, a Canadian record label with U.S. affiliates.
>
> I probably could have got it released on Warner/Reprise if I had wanted to. I *know* I could have gotten it out on Sony, for sure. But we liked the people at Linus for their enthusiasm.
>
> Right now, I've got some new songs. But life is filled with all kinds of other interests. Since I have been through my recent illness, I've got a much closer fix on what is important. My extended family is all around me, and there are a couple of them becoming teenagers that require a lot. My granddaughter is going to Ryerson Technical Institute, and my twenty-four-year-old is going into flight school. [He's also a musician too.] I'm trying to preside over that, run the business, and go to the health club. I'm a person who takes conditioning as part of the engagement. It helps everything … it helps the singing and the music.

I don't know if I have time to make another record. The isolation is the part that I am not sure about. I'm not sure that I want to bring that kind of isolation on myself again.

As much as the songs are performed on stage, it is truly a lonely occupation writing them, as any songwriter can attest to.

One thing to remember about writer's block is that every writer has experienced this problem at some point during his or her career. The first thing to do is to avoid panic. Take a few days off and do something entirely different. Go to the beach, go to the mountains, and don't try to write songs. If an idea occurs to you, write it down or put it on tape, but don't deliberately set aside time to write songs, as you might normally do.

Another possibility is to find a collaborator. Everyone I have ever known has some song ideas that are lying in notebooks or on tape that they haven't been able to finish. Find someone whose work you admire, and ask him to see if he can finish the song. Sometimes by working with another writer you will automatically be stimulated to think in new ways or to try different musical techniques that are new to you. If you already have a collaborator, and your "staleness" is partly a result of two people who know each other's ideas all too well, then find a new collaborator.

How do you find a collaborator? You can place ads through songwriters' organizations, rely upon tips from other musicians, or attend a performance by a singer/songwriter who you haven't worked with before, and see if you think her style and yours might mesh.

One other suggestion: take some music lessons. If you play finger-style guitar, study playing with a pick. If you always play with a pick, study with a finger-style player. If you've always written in a particular musical genre, study another one. Try to learn a new instrument. The musical textures of the guitar, banjo, mandolin, and piano are radically different. Each one has its own library of techniques and stylistic mannerisms. If you want to stick with the guitar, try a different kind of guitar—a nylon string, 12-string, and so forth. If you cannot afford lessons, buy an instructional DVD. Homespun Tapes has tapes of many guitar styles by outstanding players and teachers. Another possibility is to utilize different guitar tunings.

A number of singer/songwriters work in different guitar tunings, notably Joni Mitchell. When you play in a new tuning, you are not familiar with chord shapes and your fingers are apt to drift into new creative territory.

There are a number of other singer/songwriters, such as David Wilcox and Shawn Colvin, who play in a variety of guitar tunings. (Note:

Coauthor Dick Weissman has a book out called *Alternate Tunings: A Comprehensive Guide*. It comes with a CD of the musical examples.)

Another approach to writer's block is to become aware of your own work habits. If you always write in the morning, try working at night, or vice versa. Some people find that train trips or driving in a car seem to stimulate their creative juices. This has the added advantage of removing you from such distractions as phone calls and various personal commitments. If you follow this route, be sure to turn off your cell phone!

Harry Manx came to the songwriting part of the business relatively late in his musical career, but since then has been extremely prolific. It seems that when he decided what it was he needed to write about, composing was a relatively painless process for him:

> I came at songwriting thinking, up until ten years ago, that there was nothing really to say. There was sort of a certain poverty of language that wouldn't allow me to put the deeper experiences into words. So I came at it very skeptically, when I finally decided words might be the only thing we really have between us, for those who don't hear silence well. I accepted it finally, then I finally dug into it, and after the initial frustration I kind of made a breakthrough where I decided to let it flow a little more, without censoring everything I am writing. That's when I started to write some really good stuff, and now I found the approach, I guess, because recently I rented a house in Brazil by the sea. I just stayed on the laptop and wrote the whole album in that month. It didn't seem like a struggle; I was enjoying it.

So maybe I have arrived at a place where writing just happens for me.

MTV, MUSIC VIDEOS, AND PROMOTIONAL DVDS

A key promotional tool as you continue to build your audience will be a video or DVD. Some presenters care almost as much about the "look" of an artist or band as they do about the music. Festival directors and arts councils like to see how you interact with the audience in a live performance.

Like the CD, costs for doing a promotional DVD have become much more reasonable. There are video companies listed in most telephone directories that can give you a basic idea of what it will cost you to shoot, edit, and produce the kind of promotional DVD that you need.

Before you call them, be sure you have a clear idea of what you want the finished product to be. Do you want a concert video, capturing highlights and examples of how you relate to an audience? Or do you want to produce more of an MTV/VH1 kind of piece that profiles a song and your "look"? Whatever you are after, make your request clear.

It is important to mention that having a bad video with inferior audio quality is worse than not having a video at all—so plan your video project wisely and critically.

One of the most expensive parts of making a video/DVD is the editing process, which in many cases can cost as much or more than the original shoot. The good news is, there are many community colleges that now have video-editing suites and students to run them. These facilities can mean a major savings on your editing costs. The bad news is, you will be working with less experienced engineers, and your savings can well be wiped out by the extra time editing will take you at such a facility.

Just as on a CD, a more elaborate DVD project will be facilitated by having a producer to line up makeup artists, a soundman, lighting experts, or whatever else your project requires. Your DVD producer will also advise you on your performance and attempt to keep the production within your budget.

Once your production is complete, you may use it not only for promotion but also package it with an attractive cover and sell it just like you would a CD. This can potentially add to your product sales' bottom line, particularly at concerts.

There are also other ways you can create a promotional DVD for yourself. If you are performing at colleges, ask them to video the program and tell them they can use it for a class or the college television station, if you can have a copy. Most universities are happy to do this; it is training for their students and potentially programming for their station. Once you have the video, you, a friend, or a professional company can use a computer video-editing program to create a marketing DVD for yourself. It may not be a slick as a commercially done presentation, but it will be very useful to you nonetheless.

If you have had television story pieces done on you to promote an album or appearance of yours, see if you can get permission to use those for promotional purposes. You possibly can combine a number of different stories featuring both music and interview to create an interesting DVD about what you have to offer as an artist to presenters.

The world of album and artist promotion changed radically when MTV burst upon the scene in 1982. At one time, even folk, jazz, and classical artists were producing expensive videos for airplay on various television outlets (even Gordon Lightfoot produced a video for his 1980s song "Baby Step Back").

That imperative has changed, but the impact of the readily available video technology of today is a factor every professional artist has to consider.

Terry Currier of Music Millennium in Portland talks about how the entire record and music industry evolved quickly after the development of MTV:

> In the eighties MTV changed the record industry. Labels found out that they could get overnight sensation hits by making a cool little video. It didn't really equate to an artist's career; maybe that record was big and the next record didn't happen at all, sales-wise. But then the industry really started expecting that to happen, and it went from the rock side to the hip-hop side to eventually crossing over to country music, too.

When you look at the way country music used to be previous to that, your popularity on the ladder went up with time, with live performances and radio hits. Ernest Tubb dies, Webb Peirce dies, and then Johnny Cash is big and Ray Price is big. Their careers went up like a curve. They went up to a point, then went down.

INTERNET DISTRIBUTION ... CD BABY, AMAZON.COM, AND OTHER WAYS TO SELL YOUR CDS

In Chapter 4 we talked about record store distribution. Of course, there are a myriad of other ways to sell your music today.

A good place to start for the beginning recording artist is www.cdbaby.com. This is a company headquartered in Portland, Oregon, that specializes in selling the products of all sorts of musicians. You do not need to be a major player to have your CDs sold on CD Baby.

They require you to pay a small setup charge for each CD they distribute, (currently $35) and that you provide them with five for-sale CDs to start, and a sample CD to scan for the Web page they will make for you. They take a small commission from each sale they make for you, and ship them out from their warehouse.

You can sign up directly on CD Baby's Web site on the Internet or call them directly. They have an excellent reputation with artists and customers alike, and are happy to walk you through the process of getting set up with them.

Derek Sievers of CD Baby is a seemingly never-ending font of ideas about how to distribute and sell your albums, and he shares each idea with you via e-mail. It is up to you to follow up on these leads, but he has some very useful ideas and techniques.

You can find out much more about CD Baby and the prototype CD Internet distribution system at www.cdbaby.com.

Additionally, when you are registered with CD Baby, your albums are automatically available through Amazon and a variety of other companies they have reciprocal agreements with. Amazon's Web site has a special artist's section that explains how they (and many other Internet distribution sites) work (www.amazon.com).

In addition to selling your recordings through their Web presence, CD Baby has become increasingly active in pursuing digital sales, and even is now selling records through some of the giant big box stores, like Best Buy. As the years go by, inevitably digital sales on the Internet will catch up to income derived from the so-called brick-and-mortar stores.

Bear in mind, however, that simply registering with an Internet distribution company does not guarantee any additional sales. It is still up to you to create demand for the album; your product is just available in more places.

CD Baby also offers an excellent Web-hosting business, www.hostbaby. com. Your Web host provides the server that allows your Web site to float up there in cyberspace, and also provides antivirus and other protections to keep it from being infected. Hostbaby.com offers this service for $20 per month, less if you purchase multimonth packages. For that price, which is very competitive with other Web hosts, they also offer a number of services useful to a songwriter, including templates to design your own Web site, free advice on how to do so, Web statistics, Internet marketing tips, and so forth.

Almost every songwriter/performer who has a Web site offers sound samples and the opportunity to directly purchase his or her recordings from that site. There are numerous companies you can set up Web payment systems through, but one of the easiest, most secure, and universally accepted methods is PayPal. Like a credit card company, they take a small percentage for each sale processed through them (www.paypal.com).

They offer complete information on how to register with them at their site. It is a free service; no initial setup fees are required.

8

OTHER OPPORTUNITIES FOR
SONGWRITERS AND MUSICIANS

FILM

The traditional use of music in the movies was that it was a heavily orchestrated background score that accompanied the action on the screen. Different musical themes were used for different characters, and depending upon the director's vision and the composer's talent, the music could subtly underline unspoken thoughts, predict actions that would develop a few seconds or a few minutes later, bring a sense of place and time to a film, or simply directly reinforce the action. The composers were generally well-trained musicians. In the Hollywood studio system that prevailed from the inception of "talkies" in 1927 through the 1950s, another team of skilled musical orchestrators, also known as arrangers, would copy the instrumental parts from fairly extensive sketches made by the composer.

The use of songs in movies was limited, except for musicals and for cowboy movies, where such actors as Gene Autry or Roy Rogers would interrupt the action and—on or off their horses—strum their guitars and sing songs. It became obvious to the films studios and producers that if a movie had a title song, not only could the song produce an additional revenue stream, but also the listener would be reminded of the movie every time the song was played on the radio. The revenue stream could be considerable, because the song was almost always published by the film company, so income could be obtained from sheet music, sales of the soundtrack albums, or release as (hopefully) a hit single.

During the 1930s and into the 1950s, the title song was often written by two professional songwriters who were brought in to create a theme song for the movie. In other instances, the song was a collaborative effort between the composer of the film score and a lyricist. The first situation mentioned engendered some bitterness on the part of the composer of the film score, because he (and at the time it was almost invariably a male) knew very well that a hit song could bring in more revenue than the entire film score would make. Since the composer may have taken anything from four to eight weeks of highly concentrated work to compose the score, he naturally became annoyed that two songwriters could enjoy this income from working for a few hours or a few days. Some of the composers, notably Henry Mancini, fought back by cowriting the title song with a lyricist. Mancini's *Moon River* probably ultimately brought him more income than most of his film scores. Of course, an instrumental theme taken from the film score occasionally became a hit song without a lyric. Mancini's *Pink Panther* instrumental probably earned him more money than the entire group of the Pink Panther movies that featured Inspector Clouseau (Peter Sellers) as well.

Gordon Lightfoot, when talking about his work in writing for films, is somewhat ambivalent about the experience:

> It is hard to come up with the appropriate song. I have attempted to do it a couple of times. I don't think it's my bag. The only thing I wrote in that regard that worked really well was the "Canadian Railroad Trilogy" [written for a CBC special, *100 Years Young*, to celebrate Canada's centennial in 1967].
>
> I'm not good at doing stuff on commission. I wrote songs for the movie *Cool Hand Luke* that didn't get used. I wrote songs for the first Michael Douglas movie; they used the song that I liked the least of the whole lot. It's the kind of a situation whereby they fly you out there, you put down a demo, and turn around and fly back to Toronto. I could probably do that better now than I did it then. It was tough on me at that point.
>
> Another time I was at the Hollywood Roosevelt for four days writing songs for a Burt Reynolds movie called *Fade In*. I wrote the lyrics for that song, got it done, got it down; and that is how I met Terry Clements [Lightfoot's lead guitar player for the past thirty-plus years]. That's how these things happen.

By the 1980s movie studios began to realize that a movie score could be cobbled together that featured a half dozen or a dozen songs, and relegated the composer to a background role, providing filler music between the songs. *Saturday Night Fever,* released in 1977, was a highly successful movie that featured the songs of the Bee Gees. It marked the beginning of a new era in film music.

Although consigning the composer to a less important position has been a rather sad development for film composers, it has opened the floodgates of opportunity for songwriters who do not possess the formal musical skills that were part of the training of such formidable film-score heroes as Elmer Bernstein, Jerry Goldsmith, or Quincy Jones. Next time that you attend a film or watch one on television, take a look at the film credits shown at the end of the movie. You will often see a whole group of songs, and in addition to the credits for the film composer, you will see a credit for the "music supervisor." The music supervisor is generally the person who has interacted with music publishers, songwriters, and record companies that enabled a song to be used in the film.

Let's take a few minutes to discuss what all of these parties have to do with clearing the rights for the use of the song. Record companies only become involved when the original recording of a song is used in a film. The reason that a film's director and/or producer might want this to happen is that a record that is recognized by the audience sets a certain mood for the film that becomes almost a part of the film's heartbeat. The title of the song also may be the same as the title of the film, even though the two may not be directly related. For example, Solomon Burke's hit record *Stand by Me* was used in the film of the same name, even though Burke's soulful performance had little to do in terms of overall context with the tale of three boys growing up in Oregon. (Incidentally, the film and the recording were so well received that the song itself became a hit, years after its original tenure on the charts.)

If you pay attention to the use of songs in films, you will have observed that sometimes a different version of a hit song is used in a film than the one that was originally a hit. Sometimes this is a "sound-alike" version, where the producer of the new recording simply imitates the sound of the original, or it may be a very different version, with a female lead singer instead of a male, or a very different instrumental track is utilized. If the version is a sound-alike, the chances are that the film's producers simply didn't want to pay for the original recording. A bit later in this chapter, we cover some of the dollars involved in all of these procedures. For now, let's take a look at what determines the price paid to a music publisher for the use of a song in a film.

Keep in mind that in most songwriter–publisher agreements there is a 50/50 royalty split. The writer receives 50 percent of the income, and so does the publisher. If the songwriter is also the publisher of the song, he or she gets to keep 100 percent of the money. There are also several other ways of handling song royalties. If a well-known artist is also a songwriter, it is not unusual for the artist/songwriter to receive half of the publishing income, as well as the writer's money. This gives that artist/writer 75 percent of the income. The rationale that enables a publisher to accept this smaller percentage is that the writer, as an artist, offers guaranteed recordings and exposure for the songs. A music publisher must work much harder to expose songs for a songwriter who is not a recording artist without this guaranteed exposure. For the superstar artist/writer like Paul Simon or Bruce Springsteen, this exposure is automatic. Radio stations will generally feel compelled to play the new Springsteen record, while they may be hesitant to add a recording by a brand new artist.

The songwriter/artist superstar may own *all* of the songwriting and publishing rights, and simply pay a company or person a small percentage of the income to administer these rights. This means that this company simply files the copyright forms, answers requests for musical lead sheets or demos of the songs, and responds to e-mail or phone inquiries. This leaves the artist with the lion's share of the rights, but frees him or her from the responsibility of the day-to-day chores of operating a music publishing company.

Decision Time

At this point you need to decide whether you are going to attempt to promote your own music in Hollywood, or whether you will use some sort of an agent or a music publisher to do it for you. There are advantages each way, depending on your analysis of how much energy you want to put into the business aspect of publishing, how you feel about promoting yourself, and your own personality traits. It is, of course, possible to take one path, and to later shift gears and reverse your direction. For the moment, let's discuss what you have to do if you choose to promote your own music.

As we discussed in Chapter 7, the advantage of owning your own publishing is simple and obvious. You make more money! It also can be a hedge in case you run across a deal from a film producer, music publisher, or record company at a later time that necessitates your giving up publishing rights. Obviously if you don't control your own publishing rights, you can't later use these rights as a negotiating chip.

The first thing you will need to do is to develop some sort of library of music that you can submit to music supervisors. It is a good idea to have not only songs available but to also have instrumental versions of the songs, in case you run into a rush project and the singer needs to be, for example, a woman rather than a man. Of course, if you also actually write instrumental music as well, you should have some of that available on CD. It is not a bad idea to have media player files (MPs) on your computer, especially if you happen to run into a supervisor who prefers that medium. *Always* include your name, phone number, and e-mail address on anything you send out. This includes CDs, MP3s, or any written communication. Supervisors are very busy, and it is not unusual for them to want to contact someone at the last minute. If they can't find your contact information quickly and easily, they will move on to someone else.

Contacting Musical Supervisors

The obvious question that you are considering is: how do I contact a music supervisor? It doesn't take a rocket scientist to figure out that since most films are produced in Hollywood, that is where your contacts will be. This has nothing to do with where the movie is filmed, because music is the last thing that is cut into the film, and the postproduction work is *usually* done n Hollywood.

The most inexpensive source of information about music supervisors is found in quarterly issues of the Los Angeles music trade paper *The Music Connection* (see the end of this book for the address). This periodical has quarterly listings not only of music supervisors but also of music publishers and A&R personnel at record companies. Some of these people clearly indicate that they do not accept unsolicited material, and some will listen to anything that is sent to them. When sending material, keep in mind that these people are indeed busy, so if you send a 16-track CD, highlight the 3 or 4 cuts that you feel especially strongly about.

A word to the wise: Even though you have just received a contact for a music supervisor a week ago, it is always smart to check and make sure that your contact is indeed still working at the company, and that you have the correct address for that company. Nothing makes you seem more like an amateur than addressing a package to someone who no longer works for that company. It immediately indicates that you do not keep current with industry events and changes.

The Film Music Network functions in Los Angeles and New York. It holds meetings in both cities, where you may be able to meet music supervisors and other composers active in the film industry. The discussions on current issues in film scoring and copyright may also prove valuable to you.

There are a variety of tip sheets that you can subscribe to that are listed at the end of this book. They are quite expensive, and are prohibitively so for the aspiring film composer with few credits and no money. Periodicals like the *Hollywood Reporter, Variety*, and *Backstage* can help keep you abreast of movies in production and provide you with the names of people in the production process. These magazines are available by subscription, and in most cities there is at least one magazine or newspaper store that carries them alongside a rack of out-of-town newspapers.

Film editors can also be a source of jobs, because particularly in dealing with independent filmmakers and smaller-budget productions, their input and recommendations may enable you to get the assignment. (I personally got to write a score for a TV show, a movie score, and a half-dozen documentary films through the recommendation of a film editor in Denver. To show you how your network of contacts expands, the television show led to a query from another film editor that led to another film score.)

Temp Tracks

Often when a film is in production, the director or editor will insert a temporary music track into the film in order to give the director a feel for what the finished product will sound like, as well as the way it will look. If you are fortunate enough to have your song inserted into a temp track, the director may become enamored of your song, even though he was not initially planning to use it. Anyone involved in the movie industry can tell a dozen stories of entire commissioned film scores that were never used because the director never felt that they worked as well with her film as what she had used initially in her temp track.

Probably the most famous example of this phenomenon was the film *2001: A Space Odyssey,* where two film scores were commissioned (and paid for) but none matched the temp track, which happened to be *Thus Spoke Zarathustra*, a classical work by Richard Strauss.

Working outside Los Angeles

Can you get assignments for songs or score writing for movies if you live outside Los Angeles? Obviously there is a film business in New York, and prolific filmmakers Woody Allen and Spike Lee are both headquartered there. There are also many independent films that are made in other cities in the United States. When I was living in Denver, there were two or three of these each year. Of course, the budgets are much smaller, so the music budget will suffer along with everything else. Documentary films are even more spread out and are produced almost everywhere.

Working outside of Los Angeles means that the process of getting the gig is done on a somewhat more informal basis. There may be less money, but there are fewer hurdles to leap over. It is also possible that you will be able to keep the publishing rights, rather than giving them up to the company that has made the movie. This means that you can conceivably use a song for another project, whether it is a record album or another movie or a television show. This is virtually unknown in Hollywood, where giving the composer even half of the publishing is regarded as a massive concession.

Rights

The information below is intended as a general guide, and is *not* a substitute for competent legal advice. Let's assume that you are fortunate enough to get a song into a film. You will then receive a deal memo, which essentially is a one- or two-page document that precedes the issuing of a formal contract. The latter is a longer document, although nothing like the multipage recording agreements that artists suffer through. The amount that you will be paid for the use of the song depends upon a number of factors. In the film itself the music budget will be determined by:

The overall budget for the film. If the entire film has a budget of $50,000, there surely isn't going to be a healthy music budget. Some authors have estimated the music budget as about 2 to 5 percent of the total budget of the film. Remember that the music budget includes what it costs to record all the music, what the composer and arranger of any instrumental music receives, and the fees paid for the use of other songs.

The way the song is used in the film. If the song is used under the titles or the credits, it is considered to be a more important part of the film than if a fragment of the song being played on a radio appears for 30 seconds in the film. By the way, you should always insist that your song receive a title credit at the end of the film.

Typical fees for using a song in a film range from $15,000 to $60,000. If the song is extremely well known, like Paul McCartney's *Yesterday,* the fee is going to escalate way above that amount. Since there are no set fees for the use of songs in a film, it is entirely a matter of negotiations between the music publisher and the producer of the film. Richard Jay cites the use of a Metallica song for the film *Mission: Impossible 2.* The fee for licensing the band's song was a million dollars, but since the soundtrack grossed $15 million, a good time, so to speak, was had by all.

When a previously recorded version of a song is used, additional money must be paid to the record company, usually about the same amount as the producers have paid for the publishing rights. They usually split this fee 50/50 with the recording artist. If a filmmaker wanted to use *Yester-day*, the fee for licensing the Beatles' recording would undoubtedly be in the stratosphere. Other factors that determine the size of the fee include whether the complete song is used and whether it is the title song that is used at the beginning and/or end of the film. Of course, if the song used is an obscure song and only a small portion of it is used in the film, the dollars involved will be much smaller.

Is the song used more than once during the course of the film? For example, in the movie *Born Free*, there was a title song, but it was also played instrumentally on a number of occasions during the course of the film.

Aside from these considerations, the character of the uses will also be a determining factor in coming up with a fee. Some of the possible variations in rights include:

Soundtrack albums. Often, if a place on the soundtrack album is guaranteed, the music publisher (which may be you!) lowers the fee for the use of the song in the film, because there will obviously be royalties from the sales of the album. Album sales of soundtracks can be massive, as in the *O Brother, Where Art Thou?* CD, which sold more than 7 million copies, or the album based on the movie *The Titanic,* which sold more than 10 million copies. In the case of the *Titanic* score, the song "My Heart Still Goes On," as performed by Celine Dion, in addition to being a massive hit single, sold a phenomenal number of copies in sheet music. The royalties paid on soundtrack albums are usually prorated, either by the number of songs on the album or the total time of your song compared to the total time on the album, which may include both songs and instrumental selections.

Most favored nation clause. This clause states that your song can receive no less money than any other song included in the film. This is a particularly advantageous clause if you know little or nothing about the filmmaker, who may convincingly be pleading poverty while sitting on major league financing.

DVD rights. This is an increasingly important usage, as movie grosses have been going down, but the sales of DVDs are increasing.

A contract for the instrumental score for a film usually includes a provision that details how much music the composer needs to write. If the composer has made an agreement to compose and produce all the music for a set fee, more music will have to be recorded, and the higher the expenses will be in terms of paying for studio time and payments to musicians and/or vocalists. On the other hand, the longer the score is, the higher the performing rights royalties will be when (and if) the film goes on television, or is shown in European movie theaters, as explained below. In a low-budget film, a producer may try to induce the composer to write additional music after the amount agreed upon in the contract is delivered. The composer should not agree to do this without additional payment to cover additional recording, the use of more musicians and/or vocalists, and the time and energy needed to compose more music.

Other Monetary Issues and Royalties

The U.S. copyright law does not recognize performing rights in movies. You will not collect any income based on the receipts of the movie that your song appears in when it plays in American theaters. In Europe, however, performing rights societies collect between 1 and just over 2 percent of the income based on gross ticket receipts. If your movie plays in Europe, you can realize thousands of dollars in income that is not available otherwise. Oddly, the minute that your movie goes on American television, you will receive income from TV showings from ASCAP, BMI, or SESAC. Since network television is 100 percent logged by the performing rights societies, the more times the show is aired, the more income you will enjoy. In the case of local and cable television, if you are publishing your own music, you must get the producer of the movie to provide you with *cue sheets*. Cue sheets indicate where all the music appears in a film, and how long the musical cue is used.

How is it possible that movie showings don't pay performance rights in the United States? The U.S. Copyright Act lasted from 1909 to 1976. The revision process took several years, and the movie exemption from performance rights is one of the issues that were not addressed in the new law. Does it make any sense that you would receive performance income from the same song in the same movie when it comes on TV, but not in movie theaters? Probably not, but it is something that songwriters and composers have to live with, at least until the law gets changed.

Unfortunately, that change may not occur for years, if in fact it *ever* takes place.

For Hire Employment

For hire employment exists when a salaried employee of a company creates a work. It also pertains when a work is commissioned as part of a larger work, like the score of a music picture in relation to the entire movie project. The "for hire" designation, according to Shemel, Krasilovsky, and Gross's *This Business of Music*, 9th edition, "affects the initial ownership of copyright, the duration of copyright, and copyright termination rights." According to Jeffrey and Todd Brabec's *Music, Money, and Success*, 5th ed., for hire works written before 1978 are protected for

95 years. Works written from 1978 on are protected for either 95 years or 120 years from the time of creation, whichever period is shorter. When we discuss commercials, the importance of work for hire contacts will be more obvious to the reader.

Other Contacts

It is possible to make other contacts in the film world by attending film festivals and by attending the film component of the annual South by Southwest Music and Film Festival in Austin, Texas. The Sundance Film Festival in Utah offers classes in film scoring, and is a possible valuable source of contacts. ASCAP and BMI both have educational classes for aspiring film composers. The people at these organizations who work in film are also a potentially valuable source of film contacts, especially if you live in Los Angeles. It is their business to know as many people working in the film industry as possible. Whether they will help you to access these people is a function of how they assess your talent and, frankly, it is also a question of how busy they are at the time that you make contact with them. As with all other contacts, an introduction from someone they are already working with can prove helpful.

If you are interested in writing songs for films or in composing film scores, check with your local colleges or universities to see who offers a major in film. There are often student filmmakers who are looking for new music to place in their films. In most of these instances, there is not going to be any financial remuneration, so make sure that you retain the publishing rights to your songs or score.

There are a handful of agents in Los Angeles who represent composers in film. They are probably not the most fruitful outlet for someone who only writes songs, but again, building up a network of contacts always offers the potential of assisting your career.

TAXI

TAXI is a company in Los Angeles that will listen to music if you pay them a fee. They will then make recommendations as to whether your music is commercially viable, and if they believe that this is the case, they will assist you in submitting music to companies that you may never have heard of or who would not have accepted your unsolicited submission. TAXI advertises extensively in music trade papers, and their ads cite success stories of people living in out-of-the-way locations who have been able to place their songs in movies or on television. I generally object to the notion that a songwriter or composer should pay to have someone listen to their music, but if you indeed live far away from any music centers, and cannot access any contacts in the industry, TAXI is one possible avenue to get your music heard. It would be interesting to know what percentage of TAXI members have actually successfully placed their music. Given that the percentage is almost inevitably going to be small, it is not surprising that this information does not appear in TAXI's ads. To determine whether using TAXI is a viable option for you, you need to assess where you are geographically, whether you have any contacts in the industry, and whether you intend to move to Los Angeles or New York in the foreseeable future. If you are in a remote area, have no contacts, and don't plan to move, TAXI may be a useful option.

More Film Music Economics: Compensation for Film Songwriters and Composers

If you are seriously interested in this subject, you should get a copy of the most current edition of *Music, Money and Success: The Insider's Guide to Making Money in the Music Industry.* It has the most detailed information that we have encountered on the actual royalty streams that are typically available to successful songwriters and composers. Jeff Brabec is a vice president of independent music publisher Chrysalis Music, and his twin brother Todd is a longtime ASCAP vice president who works in both Los Angeles and New York. Between the two of them, there aren't many royalty deals that they haven't observed.

According to the Brabec brothers, a successful song in a movie that is a hit single, is on an album that sells two million copies, is shown abroad, performed at TV and film award shows, sells well in sheet music, is later shown on television, used as a commercial, and is a hit in foreign markets, can earn over $2 million split between the writer and publisher. (The Brabecs have a detailed breakdown of exactly what money is generated from each income source.) Another of their charts shows the song becoming part of a soundtrack album that is a worldwide hit.

For the composer who writes the score for a movie, the same authors outline a payment of $564,000, of which $250,000 comes from an initial fee, $200,000 for performance royalties (for foreign theater performances), and the remainder of the income derives from the soundtrack album and from television broadcasts.

Before you become too overwhelmed with counting your future royalties, we should also point out that the figures that the Brabecs are quoting are for major studio films. Should you get the opportunity to do a local film (as I have done), you may find yourself working with a music budget that is under $25,000. For this princely sum, you are supposed to deliver songs, background scoring, and to pay the recording studio and any additional musicians or singers that you use on the session. The good news (!) is that in both instances I was able to keep the publishing rights for my music.

You should also be aware that if you work on documentary films or "art films," the budgets are often so low as to be virtually nonexistent. If you are living in Davenport, Iowa, for example, it may be advantageous for you to accept such an opportunity, just so that you can develop a track record, and have something to play for music supervisors or film editors and directors.

Several available books warn that if you donate your services to a film that is being entered at film festivals, be careful that you have a clause in the written contract that compels the producer to renegotiate your fee if the film ends up being shown in theaters or on television. Every year there are a handful of films that begin life at these festivals and become commercially successful. You need to be careful not to give away the rights to your music in what could potentially be a successful commercial venture.

Aesthetic Issues and Power

In working on films, the vision of the composer and songwriter is always secondary to the taste and requirements of the film's director, and to a lesser extent, the producer. Your song may be a great song, but it may not "work" with the action on the screen or with the director's vision of the movie. It is a very different process than recording a song for your own album, where the artist and the producer call the shots on what is acceptable or useful. Often movie directors are not musically sophisticated, and when a composer or songwriter gives them what has been asked for, it turns out that this wasn't exactly what they really wanted. As with unused film scores, there are many amusing, if frustrating, stories about extravagant fees paid to songwriters whose work is not ever used in the finished film. On the other hand, there are examples of songs used in unsuccessful films that somehow survived the films to become popular in their own right.

TELEVISION

Dollars and Cents in Television Music

The use of music for television involves even more variables than the contracts for using music in film. At the present moment we have network television, pay television, cable television, public television, and closed circuit television.

The size of the audience for each of these mediums is different. Although cable TV has made inroads in the television marketplace, network television still has a larger share of the market and is a more lucrative medium. When a TV show decides to use a song in a show, some of the contractual terms will relate to similar matters discussed in the section on movies, such as the length of the usage in the show, the number of times it is used in a particular show, foreground versus background use, and so forth. However, the *type* of TV medium is very much a part of the negotiation in terms of the possible monetary value of the license.

In addition to these general principles, it is most important that whoever controls the rights to the song understands that if a television show has a run of four or more years, it will almost undoubtedly appear in syndication. That syndication will not only saturate the airwaves, as in the current *Law and Order* show with its many spin-offs, but the show will also appear on foreign television all over the world. So we have the possibility of:

- Network play
- Cable syndication
- Pay TV
- DVD home sales
- Possible (though unusual) television soundtrack albums
- Closed circuit television, used in specific venues like hotels

Popular public television shows, like Martin Scorsese's *Blues* series, spawned CDs, DVD and VHS copies, and even a book. The Ken Burns's TV documentaries, such as his programs on the history of jazz, have had similar ancillary distribution and generated additional revenue.

Generally, TV producers want rights for at least five years. They also often make the argument that the songwriter or composer will be able to enjoy additional income "at the back end." This refers to the fact that the performing rights organizations pay money for performances on television. If a show is run four times, your song will generate performance income each time. When the show is played in different parts of the world, you will earn additional performing rights income for those airings. Similarly, if the show goes into syndication, you will receive money from your performing rights organization for those uses.

Essentially what you need to know, if you are doing your own negotiating, is that any additional rights beyond the show itself are rights for which you should receive additional compensation. If the producer wants to use the music forever (their phrase will be "in perpetuity"), then you should receive more money. Clearly the show itself, for example, will not sell the Venezuelan broadcast rights for a flat fee.

Entertainment Lawyers

Before we discuss what sort of sums we are talking about, we should make it clear that you need to find a lawyer to represent you in the signing of the final contract. That lawyer needs to be someone who specializes in intellectual property, as opposed to a criminal lawyer or a civil lawyer who works on divorces. At the very least, you are probably going to pay $150 an hour for these services, and if you are in New York or Los Angeles, you should expect to pay at least twice that. If you cannot afford these charges because you have little or no income, you should consult the Volunteer Lawyers for the Arts. They offer legal services for little or no cost for people of limited means. They have branches in many, although not all, major cities around the country. You can contact them at www.vlany.org, or by calling their main offices in New York at 212-319-ARTS.

Television Songwriting and Composing

We have mentioned that films do not pay performance income in the United States, until the film is shown abroad or goes on American television. When music is written specifically for television, performance rights are paid on the first airing of the show and continue to be paid on subsequent showings. Because of this, and because television budgets are considerably smaller than movie budgets, the fees paid for music used on television are much smaller than what film producers pay. According to the Brabec brothers, the use of a song on a television show generally pays a synchronization fee of $1500–$3000 for a five-year license, although more money is available if other rights—such as pay TV, home videos, and cable rights—are granted. Invariably, television producers make the argument that the writer will receive considerable income "at the back end." They are referring to the performance income that is paid by BMI or ASCAP.

The fees paid may also relate to whether the song has a very specific tie-in to the show or its subject matter. A friend of mine named Otis Taylor wrote a song about Civil Rights pioneer Rosa Parks that happened to fit perfectly into a television show episode. Such a specialized use is apt to pay better than a relatively generic sort of love song, which could easily be exchanged for another similar song.

Another issue that relates to fees for both television and film music is the question of whether the film or show has already been shot and edited, or in the case of television, even aired. Randy Poe's useful book

Music Publishing cites an instance where he licensed songs for a documentary movie, knowing that the song had already been cut into the film. Because he had that information, he was able to command a larger fee for the music than a low-budget documentary film would normally be willing to pay. On occasion, television shows have already been aired with music used without licensing synchronization rights. In such a situation the songwriter is in the driver's seat, and may be able to obtain a higher than normal fee. I once had a song used in a local television show in Denver where the producers had not bothered to license the song, despite the performing group in the show mentioning to them that the song was a published and original song. I consequently received $250 for a use that I would have been happy to have granted for less than half of that amount.

In terms of the income from writing the background score for an instrumental show, the Brabecs state that ten minutes of music for each episode aired forty-four times on a network will generate an income of $68,200. They also estimate (assuming that the show is picked up internationally), that foreign royalties will be $120,000 a year, and that syndication rights will generate an additional $215,000. Over a five-year period, this amounts to $646,000. Remember that successful shows are run twice, once during the season and again at the end of the season, so that the work involved in the show is less than it might otherwise appear. Songs used for shows on cable channels will generate less income both in terms of the synchronization rights and the performance income. Music fees for one-hour shows pay more than the fees for half-hour shows, because they obviously demand more work from the composer than the shorter shows.

Part of the reluctance of television producers to pay higher synchronization fees is that most television shows actually cost more to produce than the network pays for them. It is only when the show goes into syndication, usually after four years, that the producers actually start to earn money.

Title Themes or Songs

The real money in composing for television is when a song or an instrumental theme becomes closely associated with a show and is used during the entire run of the show. For a show that continues to be popular, the run might be five to ten years. Even though the composer may have moved on to other shows, the title song continues to be played, and the composer/songwriter continues to earn performance income. For example, a show like *The Rockford Files* has appeared on countless cable TV transmissions, with its catchy and recognizable music theme.

If you examine the credits for TV music, you will notice that some composers have written five or six themes, and then have moved on to other shows and additional themes. They often follow the practice of writing the theme and the first few episodes, and then moving on to other assignments.

THEATER

Grand Rights: Writing Music for Plays

Grand rights are the rights that govern the use of music in the theater. They are quite different from the rights that govern the use of music on records or in film and television. Grand rights are paid as a percentage of the gross income from shows that run in a theater, and they are governed by the Dramatist Guild. The fee usually paid is 6 percent of the gross, which is split between three parties—the composer of the songs, the lyricist of the songs, and the writer of the "book" or script. For Broadway shows, the vast majority of shows separate the functions of the lyricist and the person who composes the tunes, although there are exceptions, notably Stephen Sondheim. It is not unusual for the lyricist to be the same person who writes the lyrics to the song.

When you consider that many Broadway shows entail a minimum ticket price of $100, that the successful shows often spawn touring companies, and there may also be productions in London and other locales, the income generated by a hit show can be enormous. The most extreme example of the value of these rights is probably the show *Phantom of the Opera*. At the current writing, in early 2007, the show has been running since 1988(!), making it the longest running Broadway show of all time. The New York gross of the show, according to the *New York Times,* is just short of $600 million. This means that the grand rights have generated about $36 million! This does not include income from the many touring shows, the soundtrack album, and the inevitable dinner theater and local college productions that will continue to occur for the next generation. Of course, for every *Phantom*, there are a thousand shows that never even get produced, not to mention the shows that die in out-of-town tryouts or the ones that open and close in a matter of days or weeks.

Phantom is a musical, and shows that involve background music are paid at considerably less generous rates, usually with small flat fees for each performance.

When the authors of a show make an agreement with a producer, the producer pays a fee for optioning the show, listed by the Brabecs as

$18,000 for a twelve-month option. There are also small advance payments, usually up to $60,000 for the rehearsal period, and one fee of $4500 for full performance weeks in out-of-town tryouts. The 6 percent figure only comes into play when the show has recouped its original investment, which many shows never succeed in doing.

Practical Matters

If you become involved in writing songs or music for a local show—in, say, Omaha or Denver—the chances are that you will receive comparatively little (or nothing) in the form of advance payments. It is essential that you retain the publishing rights to any songs that you have written for the show, in case you ever want to use these songs for other purposes, such as your own recordings. If you give up the rights, if you ever produce your own recording, you will find yourself in the unpleasant and awkward position of having to pay a publisher for songs that he owns but which have never generated any income for you.

Other Opportunities for Writing Music for the Theater

Many opportunities may exist in terms of writing music for the theater. Churches sometimes commission shows that commemorate specific religious holidays, local theaters may ask you to write original music or songs, and conventions of unions or other organizations sometimes use original music to provide entertainment or educational information for their members. It is impossible to provide specific information about what to charge for such commissions, but some of the factors you may want to look at are:

- How large is the organization and what kind of money does it have to spend?
- Will the audience pay to attend the event?
- How much time will it take for you to write the material?
- Are the songs completely specific to the play or meeting, or do they have any commercial value beyond the event? If so, you certainly want to retain the music publishing rights.

Will the show ever be presented again? If so, is there some provision to pay you some sort of reuse fee?

WRITING COMMERCIALS

There are tremendous variations in compensation for writing commercials. Most of the factors are reasonably obvious. Is the commercial being used by a local diner, by an internationally famous beer company, or by a regional grocery chain? Is the commercial going to air on radio, television, or both?

The music for the bulk of commercials that we see on network television is written and recorded in New York, simply because New York is the home base of most major advertising agencies, and music is the last thing that is cut into commercials. Although a sizeable amount of national work is done in Chicago, Los Angeles, Nashville, Dallas, and in various regional markets like Kansas City or Denver, New York is still the center of most of the action.

During the past ten years, the music for commercials has changed in several ways. Fifteen or twenty years ago, there was a characteristic vocal "jingle" sound of four or five voices, often with each singer recording three or four times. At present there are far less sung jingles and more instrumental ones. Another fundamental difference in musical style is that jingles sound increasingly like current pop-rock records, rather than having a sort of 1950s smooth vocal pop-jazz sound. All through the 1960s, rock and roll may have dominated the airwaves, but not when it came to jingles. An older vocal sound prevailed, and the music was much more conservative. Over the years, the sound of commercials has come much closer to the sound of current records. Because there are less sung jingles, the importance of always putting the vocals way out front and having them be clearly audible has changed to identifying the product through graphics or the spoken voice.

Commercials and Money, Union and Nonunion

The bad news for composers writing music for commercials is that they don't make as much money as vocalists do. Composing music for commercials has never paid residuals to the composer. Residuals are repayment income enjoyed by singers and musicians when commercials are run repeatedly. Because composers have never been paid in this way, most of the jingle composers of the 1960s through the 1980s either sang on commercials or at least put their names on the union contracts. Singers could (and can) earn as much as $100,000 for an hour's work singing for a national product, provided that product chooses to saturate the airwaves with its ads. Musicians also earned residuals for playing on commercials, although their earnings are much lower. They are paid every thirteen weeks that a commercial is aired. The amounts paid to vocalists are affected by whether the commercial is aired in prime time and whether it is bought as a local, regional, or national commercial. I have personally played on recording sessions where composers lip-synced—not actually singing anything, but doing enough to merit their being placed as singers on the contract.

I witnessed other sessions where the composer did sing, but where their weak vocals had to be compensated for by the skilled professional singers on the session. Now it may strike you that $100,000 is an outrageous amount of money to pay a singer for an hour's work, but keep in mind that it is a pittance compared to what it will cost to buy 30 seconds of TV time. The Super Bowl, which has a guaranteed massive audience, is currently charging more than $2 million dollars for 30 seconds of airtime. The 2006 Winter Olympics charged a mere $700,000 for 30 seconds.

The amounts of money charged for airtime on network shows vary depending on the time of day that the commercial is broadcast and the success of a particular show. The higher the audience ratings for the show, the more expensive the time will cost. Suddenly $100,000 does not seem like so much money!

When commercials are done nonunion, there are no residual payments, and the singers and musicians get one flat payment for a commercial that may literally be run for years. The composers remain in the same position—they get one fee, period. (It should be mentioned that a number of jingle composers are fine musicians, play in their own recording sessions, or conduct the orchestra. Under those circumstances, they do receive residuals on union recording sessions.)

In major jingle markets, the way that the jingle business works is that an advertising agency sends out a call, asking for independent music houses to come up with a campaign for a particular product. Sometimes the call indicates the use of a company logo or it even may contain lyrics written by an agency copywriter.

Sometimes a minimal amount of money is offered for doing these jingle demos. The winning music house then gets to produce and record the jingle. Usually someone from the agency attends the session and supervises the proceedings.

As is the case with movies, agency producers often have a minimum knowledge of music and they tend to speak in broad generalities. This places the composer in the position of having to guess what the advertising people actually mean. To cite an extreme, absurd example, I was once playing banjo on a commercial that was not going too well because the violin player could not play the sort of country hoedown style that the client wanted. The agency person walked into the studio and asked me whether I could play a "Latin-Eddie Peabody, bluegrass-rock sound." Now Eddie Peabody was an extremely flashy ragtime-ish Dixieland kind of banjo player, and bluegrass is played on a different sort of banjo, the 5-string; Latin music generally does not utilize banjos, and neither does rock and roll. Since I had already been playing on jingles for a few years, I smiled at the agency person and said, "No problem." It was obvious to me that he didn't know what he was talking about, but simply wanted to be reassured that he was going to have some input into the process.

Local and Regional Jingles

In the local and regional music markets, there may be no middleman—just the advertising agency and the composer. In cities like Denver, it is not unusual for a agency to record a jingle that is used in the Rocky Mountain region. For composing a regional jingle, the fees will be in the $2500 to $20,000 range, depending upon the product and budget. Local commercials for a single market or public service announcements will pay much less. If you look in your local phone book, you will see a surprising number of advertising agencies, but some only deal with print ads for newspapers or magazines. To break into this work as a composer, you need to make a CD of very short examples of music in different styles. You can never tell what sort of music they will be looking for. Although record companies prefer a specific and consistent image in their artists, advertising agencies are willing to accept more versatility on the part of their preferred composers.

Jingles and the Record Companies

There is nothing in the copyright law that indicates a specific fee for the use of a song in a jingle campaign. Fees have to be negotiated between the agency and the music publisher. If the original recording of a song is used, just as with a movie use, an additional fee must be negotiated with the record company. Fees have gone as high as a million dollars for the use of a song in a commercial. A number of factors influence the fee, including whether the jingle will be shown on both radio and television, whether the agency wants contractual assurance that the song will not be used as a commercial for a similar product, or whether it wants total exclusivity that ensures that the song will not be used as a commercial for any other product at all.

If the song has to endure lyric changes, the publisher may ask for more money because he will maintain that this will decrease the value of the song, because it will become too closely identified with a product. Giant hit songs by superstars cost more to license than a commercial by an unknown generic rock or country group. In fact, if the agency uses a comparatively unknown group, the agency may try to reduce the amount of the synchronization license in exchange for flashing the name of the group on the screen during the commercial.

During the 1960s, it was considered uncool for rock groups to allow their music to be used as commercials, but currently it seems to be in vogue, with everyone from Bob Dylan to Bob Seger transforming their hit songs into commercials. My personal favorite, in the irony department, is Graham Nash's lyrical *Teach Your Children* being used in an underwear commercial. It is entirely up to you as to whether you want to explore the world of commercials or if you choose to avoid this particular outlet for your musical talents.

OPPORTUNITIES FOR MUSICIANS WITH MUSIC PRINT PUBLISHERS

Traditionally the term "music publishing" meant sheet music. During the 1920s and up until the rock and roll revolution, most people learned music from printed piano music. During the 1920s and 1930s there were piano players in the five-and-dime stores that demonstrated the music by playing it live in the store. If the customers liked what they were hearing, they purchased the sheet music. Country music and early blues were seldom published in sheet-music form, and the people who played it either wrote it themselves or learned it from recordings by ear. When rock and roll came along, the sheet music market was greatly diminished, because most of the music was relatively easy to pick up, and most people learned the music by ear rather than from notation. The demand for printed music continued for school bands and choruses, but the income from the sales of sheet music was dwarfed by the monies available from record royalties and performance rights.

Certain markets did open up in the world of sheet music, especially in the world of instructional materials for the guitar. Until the 1950s there were relatively few guitar methods available, but a guitar player from St. Louis named Mel Bay created a six-volume guitar instruction method, and ended up publishing it himself when other music publishers assured him that there was no market for a new guitar method. Incidentally, over the years, the method has sold millions of copies, and spawned the birth of Mel Bay Publications, a large music print company now operated by Mel's son, Bill Bay.

Because sheet music represented an important market, for years there were dozens of sheet-music publishers, mostly headquartered in New York. As sheet-music sales were dwarfed by other income sources, many of the print music companies went out of business. Today there are five major players in the field: Hal Leonard, Alfred Music, Music Sales, Carl Fischer, and Mel Bay. Music Sales and Carl Fischer are New York companies, but Mel Bay remains in suburban St. Louis, Hal Leonard is in Milwaukee, and Alfred is in Los Angeles. Some other publishers, like Cherry Lane, Theodore Presser, and Sher, remain active but are distributed by the companies above, in much the same way that many of the independent record labels are distributed by the major labels.

If you own your own publishing and have a hit record, you will need to license the rights to one of these five companies to print the actual sheet music. For further information, you can consult the references at the end of this book. The rest of this section deals with opportunities available for musicians to create instructional materials for the print publishers.

Creating Instructional Materials

If you go to a local music store that has a reasonable stock of printed music, you will be amazed at the number of instructional books that are available. Since piano and guitar are the two most popular instruments, you will notice that an amazing number of instructional books are available. These books tend to fall into several categories. They are: method books, collections of solos, mixed folios, and "off the record" solos.

Method books are step-by-step instructional books designed to teach the prospective student how to play an instrument. Collections of solos are original pieces for an instrument. These are often new pieces written in the style of successful artists. Other examples are solos designed to teach a particular instrumental technique. Mixed folios include works by various composers or songwriters mixed together. Off-the-record solos are transcriptions of recorded solos.

There is a constant demand for instructional books, and they represent a source of income for the musician that can be done at home rather than on stage. Typically the royalties paid on these instructional books are 10 percent of the retail selling price of the book, sometimes reduced to a smaller percentage when the publisher offers special discounts for quantity orders. Incidentally, print publishers tend to pay these royalties scrupulously, in intervals of three to twelve months, depending upon which publisher you are dealing with. Some publishers offer small advances, usually up to $500, half of which is paid upon signing of a contract, and the other half on acceptance of the manuscript or its actual publication.

You are probably wondering whether you can actually earn any money from writing instructional books. The answer is a definite yes, although it is not possible to predict the success of a prospective book. I have written some instruction books that have remained in print for twenty-five years, and others that sold decently for four or five years and then were taken out of print.

There are a few books, like the John Thompson piano method, that have been in print for well over fifty years, and have been translated into more than a dozen foreign languages. One of my favorite examples of striking the mother lode with an instructional book is the Roger d'Filiberto electric bass method, published by Mel Bay. It was the first method for electric bass that hit the marketplace, and it ended up selling over a million and a quarter copies. The book was originally sold at a list price of $2.98, and later raised by a dollar—and the royalties earned by the author at a 10 percent royalty have exceeded $350,000! All for a modest and rather short book that I suspect the author wrote in a week or two.

The Public Domain

If you take a good look at many of the available method books, you will note that they often include old songs like *Go Tell Aunt Rhody* or *Down in the Valley*, as opposed to contemporary rock or country songs. The reason for this is quite simple. If you use songs that are in the current repertoire (we'll explain what that means shortly), you need to license the songs from whoever published them. Your 10 percent royalty will then be shared with these other songwriters. If you include five original songs and five songs by other composers, then your 10 percent royalty will be reduced to 5 percent. Even worse, if you are doing your book for one of the five publishers listed above and the song you want has been licensed to a different print publisher, you may not even be able to use the song.

For these reasons, most of the tunes used in instructional books are either new tunes by the author of the book or they are songs in the public domain. Currently the copyright law protects songs for the life of the last surviving author, plus seventy years. Songs written before the new Copyright Act of 1978 are protected for ninety-five years from the date of publication. Now you know why a tune like *Bicycle Built for Two*, an 1890s golden oldie, might find its way into a rock and roll instruction book. Incidentally, many instructional authors combine the best of both worlds by writing pieces in the style of a particular artist. These cannot be exact copies of the original composer's work, but they often are obviously somewhat similar to what the original composer wrote. Every songwriter or composer has his or her own stylistic mannerisms, and it is legitimate to copy the mannerism, and even to title the piece "in the style of —." Be careful, however, not to copy specific melodies or lyrics, or you will be in violation of the Copyright Act, and will probably get sued.

Selling Instructional Material

In order to convince a print publisher to put out a new book, you need to write at least a sample chapter of the book, and include a table of contents and an estimate of how long the book will be. It is also a good idea to include a market analysis that explains why there is a market for your book and how it differs from material that already is in the marketplace. Of course, the more books you are able to get published, the more credibility you have as an author and the more contacts you will develop in the music print world. In general, I have found that it is relatively easy to access music print publishers, and they are much more responsive to proposals than record companies tend to be.

It is also possible to publish your own materials, given the prevalence of computers and computerized music programs. The only problem you will have is the same one that you experience when you produce and market your own recordings: Do you have a way of distributing the product, outside of the immediate area that you live in? It is also possible to make distribution deals, where you enlist one of the major publishers to distribute your products, but you retain control over the physical creation of the product. A friend of mine named Ron Greene from Durango, Colorado, created charts of chords for a variety of instruments. He initially marketed them himself, but later farmed out the distribution of the product to the print division of Warner Brother Music, which is now owned by Alfred Music.

Other Instructional Opportunities

There is a steady demand for music arrangers in the world of printed music. Arrangers are paid flat fees, because they are either transcribing material from recordings or they are rearranging melodies written by other composers for a new group of instruments. As long as schools have bands and choral groups, there will be a demand for well-trained musicians who have these skills. Arrangers usually charge on a per-page basis, and a few arrangers are on staff at print publishers, doing their work in the office of the publisher. There is a constant demand for simplifying existing music so that a rank amateur can play something resembling the original piece.

CD and DVD Instructional Material

Many of the print publishers now include CDs or DVDs inserted into their books or as stand-alone units. Homespun Tapes and Hot Licks are two companies that specialize in video instructional materials. They generally include some written instructional materials with the recordings, but the focus is on the video aspects, including such details as how the player holds the instrument.

Most competent musicians have developed interesting instrumental techniques. Sharing them in the form of instructional videos, CDs, and books is gratifying, and can be an excellent source of additional income for the musician. Be sure that your material is playable by students. Many of the CDs that accompany instruction books utilize tempos that are too fast for the average student.

PRODUCTION LIBRARIES

Production libraries are companies that offer music for use in commercials, low-budget movies, and the like. The key to the use of production libraries lies in the term "low budget." The libraries put together music that might suit any conceivable use—for example, up-tempo fiddle tunes, hard rock solos, and so forth—so that the client can preview the music and pay a "needle drop" fee for each use. These fees are modest, usually in the $75 to $100 range. It is possible to construct a commercial with music that includes virtually no monetary expense. That is the good news for the client. The bad news is that the music invariably sounds a bit on the generic side, particularly since the consumer is quite likely to have heard the music used before for another product. Whether the client considers this as a negative thing is a matter of taste and opinion.

Production libraries can be found all over the United States. Some of their music is even of symphonic proportions, usually recorded by nonunion orchestras in other parts of the world.

If you have a home studio and either play a bunch of instruments or have a synthesizer with instrumental samples, you may want to sell some of your music to a production library. There are also companies in various parts of the United States that do radio station identifications (IDs) and commercials that are known as drop-ins. Radio station IDs are usually sold as exclusive to a particular city or metropolitan area, so that the consumer can associate a particular station with a specific musical ID. Drop-ins are commercials that use the same instrumental bed but have different vocals that are keyed to a particular product. For example, a Chevrolet dealer in Denver might use the same drop-in commercial as a Ford dealer in Omaha. In each case, the name of the company and its location are dubbed in over an existing instrumental track.

Radio station IDs and drop-in commercials are low-budget items. They are generally done without union contracts, and the talents either get a flat fee or they are on staff with the production company and earn a regular salary for this work.

NEW MEDIA

In the last few years a number of new outlets have developed for song-writers and composers. They include video games and ring tones. According to the Brabec brothers, ring-tone licenses typically are offered in the one- to three-year range. As with movie or television rights, the company that wants the license will endeavor to get a license for world-wide use, and the publisher will probably try to restrict the territory of the license to North America. This is a critical matter, because ring tones have been in widespread use in Asia for some time, so that the Asia rights are particularly lucrative.

Royalties are typically ten cents for each completed download of a composition to a cell phone, although they can also be paid as a per-centage of the income earned by the cell phone company from the use of the composition. If the ring tones are being generated by a company's computer, a flat fee is required. Other matters to be negotiated are the maximum length of the ring tone, any rights for public performance, and as with movie songs, possible most favored nation clauses.

Video games have become increasingly popular, and composing music for video games is particularly demanding because it is not pos-sible to estimate how long the player of the games will take to play the game. Royalties can be structured per composition used, or buyouts at varying fees can be negotiated. Since some video games end up sell-ing in the millions, the composer and publisher should be cautious about agreeing to buyouts. Recently video game purveyors have taken to using music by unknown or little-known composers or rock groups, and offering buyouts at relatively low prices, like $2500. As is so often the case, the game company will argue that the use of the tune will provide the little-known artist with extensive exposure. (We have often wondered how many musicians have died from exposure!) Whether this exposure will result in consequent record sales is questionable.

9

REASONS FOR IT ALL
The Lovin' of the Game

If you have read the book all the way to this point, you now know that being a songwriter/performer is an incredibly demanding, competitive, complicated undertaking (if you are not already working at doing it yourself, in which case you were already more than aware of that!).

Why would someone put himself or herself through so much, for no guarantee of financial gain or security?

The answer to that question is as individual as the artist is unique; for myself, nothing can compare to the shiver that runs up your spine when you know a song of yours truly connects with an audience (an unfailing barometer of audience emotion, I believe). And there is the joy of completing a creative project, whether it is a song, album, or even a commercial jingle, and the freedom of knowing that you work for yourself, using your own experience, talent, and motivation to succeed.

There are songs I have written people have used in marriage ceremonies, other songs of mine people have used for funerals, and my instrumental compositions have been used in churches and to sell plumbing supplies and other commodities. Each time a piece is used, I am honored, flattered, or amused; I cannot imagine that working in an office cubicle somewhere (though it most probably would have better benefits) would be quite as interesting or fulfilling.

Harry Manx talks about similar motivations for continuing to write and perform his songs:

> It's the moments when people come up to me and tell me how the music impacts their lives. People getting married to the music,

165

people being touched in some way. The fact that it reaches people, that's enough for me. I'm happy to drive a nice car because of it, that's on the fiscal level. But if I wasn't getting that kind of feedback from folks, I don't know how much I would be willing to do it.

As a songwriter/performer, I have had to spend much of my life traveling and another sizable percentage of my working life onstage. It has given me everything that has been wonderful about my life, including lifelong friends, romantic relationships, and a deep respect for the history, beauty, and diversity of this continent.

I remember one particular very early morning, driving south from the Montana border, somewhere close to Meeteetse, Wyoming. I had done a successful concert the night before, but had awakened about 5 A.M. and set out for the next gig. As the sun came up over Wyoming 125—one of the loneliest roads in the United States—an early morning shower had just concluded and the sun began streaming through the dissipating cloud layers. I hadn't seen another car in either direction for over an hour.

The sky turned twenty shades of purple, then shades of blue, then of orange and red, the clouds and moisture in the atmosphere heightening the kaleidoscope-like effect in the crystal-clear Wyoming air. It was a magical sight unlike any I had ever seen before, and I was so grateful to my songs and music that they had taken me there and allowed me to experience it. Moments like that, and countless other unforgettable vignettes, are why I have persevered in this lifestyle for so long.

Gordon Lightfoot has focused many of his songs around themes of natural beauty and geography, so when I asked him about his fondest memories as a performer, I was not surprised when he said:

> There have been many great venues. There was a trip to Australia, three trips to Europe. We played the Royal Albert Hall in London three times. We played the Universal Amphitheatre, the Greek Theatre, even the Hollywood Bowl; plus four consecutive engagements at the Lincoln Center in New York. We did that through the seventies, and it became the place we played in New York.
>
> All those venues might pale when I think about my trip to perform in Anchorage or Fairbanks. I'll never forget the night we played in Fairbanks, and it will stay with me all of my life—what a thrill it was up there in the land of the midnight sun.
>
> We just played in a school there.... I don't know what it was that made the night so special, but it was.

My son, Dylan, was immersed in music from the time he was born, and he has developed into a fine bass guitar player. His musical interests are different (and much more diverse) than my own, but he maintains a love for the music his dad put him through as a youngster. It has been rewarding to have him join me on bass at festivals and concerts, when he has the opportunity and inclination to do so. As a songwriter and/or performer, your children and family will also appreciate (or just endure) your aspirations and striving.

Eliza Gilkyson talks about this being one of the rewards of the life she has lived and also talks about when she really learned to be thankful for the professional life she had:

> I've had some moments in the last few years, having my son perform with me, having him become so involved in music ... that has been very meaningful to me. Somehow, as horrible a parent as I sometimes thought I was, because I was very selfish about pursuing music and not creating more security for my family, just knowing that the kids still want to play music and be part of it [makes it worthwhile].
>
> There have been some times, doing a song like "Requiem," where people who don't know me, where I have felt like I have my place in the world.
>
> The thing I realized after I knew I was not going to be the next biggest "whatever" was that I realized that I wanted my own booth in the marketplace. I didn't care if it was the gold leaf booth. Somehow, in the last few years, that has happened for me. People are receptive to what I have to say, and all of the struggles I had to find my voice have actually brought me to kind of a unique voice that is just mine. All those years I was trying to be like somebody, I didn't find my own voice until I let go of that.

It is difficult to keep both your songs and your attitude fresh after being in this profession for a few years or a few decades, but it is an essential part of being able to make the music work, night after night. Joni Mitchell, after having requests shouted at her, alluded to that when she once remarked onstage:

> That's always been a difference between being a visual artist and a performer—the artist paints a picture, people look at it, somebody buys it or maybe no one buys it, but it's done. No one ever said to Van Gogh, "Paint a 'Starry Night' again, man."

I often use a technique similar to that of actors on stage who are trying to keep lines they recite night after night new. I try to remember where I was, what was on my mind, or what inspired me at the time I wrote the song, or I attempt to recollect how that song made me feel when I began playing it, or try to remember a specific rendition of the song in a place where it really worked.

I am acutely aware that, as primarily a solo performer, it is totally up to me to induce the audience to respond to the song. Sometimes the responses can be surprising and not at all what you expect—but that is part of the excitement of live performance.

Occasionally, no matter what you do, you will find a flat audience that doesn't get the songs, doesn't like or understand the jokes, and can't figure out what you are doing up there!

About twenty years ago I was booked into a little Nebraska bar in ranching country by a fellow who really liked my music, and thought he would be doing me a favor by having me come and play at his place on a Saturday night. Now, the people in rural Nebraska can be warm, witty, and friendly, but the phrase "culturally progressive and open-minded" is not often used to describe that region.

As I walked in the bar to set up that evening, I knew I was in for a long night when all the heads with feed caps turned to stare at me as I entered the door, with that "Who are you and what the hell are you here for?" look.

The rest of the night was pretty much as I expected, essentially working as background music for pool games and sexist comments about the girls who would appear from time to time on the television.

I did overhear one bit of priceless conversation, however. One older rancher at the bar, nursing his fourteenth or so beer, turned to his buddy and said, pointing at me as I was singing some song I believed in, "Why would any son of a bitch want to do that?"

It was actually a good question, and one I have been asking myself ever since. Answering that question is also part of the reason for writing this book.

However, no matter how frustrating or clueless the audience or listeners may sometimes be, we have to be ever appreciative they are there. It is hard to keep in mind that as old and as often played your songs may seem to you, there are always people in your audience listening to your music for the very first time, and they deserve your best effort. You probably wouldn't bother to play that same song of yours that you wrote five years ago again if they were not there.

Eliza Gilkyson says about audiences, songwriting, and the satisfaction she derives from her art:

> The writing of a song is so personal, and that is very cathartic. But it is putting it in front of people that make it what it is. I wouldn't sit around and play that same song over and over again if there

weren't people in front of me. I would be bored and not very satisfied. The mirroring from people is what gives the song life again and again.

All the aspects of the life are interwoven. I think that they all are very rewarding and I feel nothing but lucky to get to do this. Of all the things to do in the world, this is the one that, for me, is the most fun, rewarding, and fulfilling.

This book contains a lot of sound business advice, tips, and suggestions as regards the music business, but I believe it is important that we never lose sight that music is far more than business: it is magic, and has the power to change people's lives for the better. I wrote a song a few years ago called "Its Own Reward" about that subject—that most of the things that we do that turn out well for us happen because we do them for their own sake. We have not done those tasks to produce money, love, material goods, or fame. (Though if we are to survive as professional songwriters and performers, those obviously have to be by-products!) Hopefully we do the music and sing the songs with the message and impact of our art in mind.

Harry Manx believes this is one of the secrets of your songs connecting with the audience:

> We can always put the music first, ahead of ourselves. If the focus is on the music, if it's more about the music than it is about you, then the people will feel that. If you do that, I think it will lead you into a good solid career, because people will love what you do.

I wrote in an earlier chapter about how I feel it is important to listen to other practitioners of this art/craft of writing songs, in order to educate yourself on styles and traditions of music and melody you are writing, and to educate your ears on what great songs sound like.

Though I still believe this, there is a definite danger in becoming too critical of your own work and of not moving through the steps of writing bad songs to get to the point of writing good songs, because you believe nothing you write will ever match the songs of artists you admire.

In his early years, no less of a songwriting legend than Gordon Lightfoot wrote dozens of songs that he hopes will never see the light of day. I have many early efforts as well that I would prefer any listeners who enjoy my music not judge me by. But the rules of the process (for most of us) are similar to being an apprentice in a trade: you have to make mistakes and produce inferior work before you can become a master. For most of us, there is no way of shortcutting this process. The only mistake is to not finish a song because you don't think it is good enough. Finish it and move on to the next one.

Eliza Gilkyson has moved through all of those stages of development in her songwriting life, and advises songwriters:

> If people can just find that place within themselves where they are pushing their own self-awareness via music, then they can keep growing. People get discouraged, because they think "someone out there already wrote this" or "they already have years of writing and playing under their belt." I think each person has something unique to offer, and the element of self-discovery is what makes something fresh and inspiring to others. We all have come up with the same chord progressions, the same licks, [and] there are elements in other people's process in everything we do. But there is something about stumbling across it for yourself—an idea, a thought, or a chord progression—that gives it an element of newness. If it's your discovery, then somehow it is uniquely yours. I don't think people should be discouraged about what has gone on before them, and they should continue to find their own edge and what's there for them.

I am ever mindful of how fortunate I am to do this art/craft for a living. Though it has been frustrating, competitive, and sometimes annoying, it offers great freedom and a chance to make an individual mark in a increasingly homogenized corporate world. Sometimes, when I am having a difficult night, I try to remind myself that there are hundreds of people who would trade their lifestyles for mine (though on nights like that, it's hard to imagine why).

As in the rest of life, however, with great freedom comes great responsibility. The usual tasks and perquisites assumed by employers on behalf of their workers are not there, unless you put them in place for yourself. I have come to believe that writing and performing the songs is the smallest part of the job. I have also heard songwriter/performers refer to themselves as "professional drivers and roadies, [carrying equipment] who then play the music for free." There have been many of my own tours where I would heartily agree with them.

However, there is no denying the magic of a good night when the songs are going well and the audience is raptly listening, clapping along, or otherwise responding to the tenor of the song. When the strings feel like silken strands under your fingers, and you can hit that high note you wrote in a song twenty years ago because you feel the electric charge of the listeners—you know that at that second, you are exactly in this world where you were meant to be.

It is an interesting phenomenon that most songwriter/performers find every triumph bittersweet. "Where am I going to find the inspiration and story to write my next song?" "Will the audiences like it as much as the other songs of mine they enjoy?" "Will my voice still be pleasing and listenable when I am older?" These are hard questions that temper the satisfaction of achieving success in this endeavor.

Still, when that second encore is requested by a crowd that is giving you a standing ovation, when a short letter comes in the mail that says a song of yours has helped someone's mother get through cancer chemotherapy treatments, or when an e-mail comes from a distant foreign country asking you the chord progression of a song you wrote—you know at least some of the sacrifices you have made to be a songwriter/performer are worth it.

Maine singer/songwriter David Mallet once wrote a song called "The Road Goes on Forever." That pretty well describes this lifestyle kind of artistic choice. There is no clear-cut beginning, and hopefully no dead ends. You keep writing, performing, practicing your instrument, booking the gigs, promoting the songs, doing the traveling, doing the best you can. If you are totally committed, and write and perform the music for its own sake, there is no telling where that road will take you.

Gordon Lightfoot pretty well sums all this up when he advises all of us to:

Work hard and keep your discipline together. Keep writing, and mind you don't get off on a tangent. You have to have some self-control in this business. Don't let your guitars sag, and keep them in tune ... and keep on practicing.

BIBLIOGRAPHY AND
MUSICIAN RESOURCES

BOOKS

Adams, Ramsay, David Hantliuk, and David Weiss. *Music Supervision: The Complete Guide to Selecting Movies, TV, Game, and New Media*. New York: Schirmer Trade Books, 2005.

Beall, Eric. *Making Music Make Money: An Insider's Guide to Becoming Your Own Music Publisher*. Boston: Berklee Press, 2004.

Borg, Bobby. *The Musician's Handbook: A Practical Guide to Understanding the Music Business*. New York: Billboard Books, 2003.

Brabec, Jeffrey, and Todd Brabec. *Music, Money and Success: The Insider's Guide to Making Money in the Music Industry*. New York: Schirmer Trade Books, 2004.

Braheny, John. *The Craft and Business of Songwriting*. 3rd ed. Cincinnati: Writer's Digest, 2006.

Casola, Mary. *The Independent Working Musician*. Vallejo, CA: Mix Books, 1998.

Citron, Stephen. Songwriting. New York: William Morrow, 1985.

Coxson, Mona. *Some Straight Talk about the Music Business*. 2nd ed. Toronto: CM Books, 1986.

Curran, Mark. *Sell Your Music; The Musician's Survival Guide to Direct Distribution on the Internet*. Simi Valley, CA: NMD Books, 2001.

Davis, Sheila. *Successful Lyric Writing: A Step-by-Step Course*. Cincinnati: Writer's Digest, 1988.

Davison, Mark. *All Area Access Personal Management for Unsigned Musicians*. Milwaukee: Hal Leonard, 1997.

Frascogna, Xavier M., Jr., and H. Lee Hetherington. *Successful Artist Management*. 4th rev. ed. New York: Billboard Publications, 2004.

Frith, Simon, and Lee Marshall, eds. *Music and Copyright*. 2nd ed. New York: Routledge, 2007.

Gillette, Steve. *Songwriting and the Creative Process*. Bethlehem, PA: Sing Out! 1999.

Goldberg, Justin. *The Ultimate Survival Guide to the New Music Industry: Handbook for Hell*. Hollywood: Lone Eagle, 2004.

Goldstein, Jeri. *How to Be Your Own Booking Agent*. Rev. ed. Charlottesville, VA: New Music Times, 2004.

Gordon, Steve. *The Future of the Music Business: How to Succeed with the New Digital Technologies*. San Francisco: Backbeat Books, 2005.

Hall, Tom T. *The Songwriter's Handbook*. Nashville: Rutledge Hill Press, 1987.

Halloran, Mark, ed. *The Musician's Business and Legal Guide*. Upper Saddle River, NJ: Prentice Hall, 2001.

Haring, Bruce. *How Not to Destroy Your Career in Music: Avoiding the Common Mistakes Most Musicians Make*. Los Angeles: Lone Eagle, 2005.

Heflick, David. *How to Make Money Performing in Schools*. Orient, WA: Silcox Productions, 1996.

Hollywood Music Industry Directory. Hollywood: JM Northern Media, 2005.

Jay, Richard. *How to Get Your Music in Film and TV*. New York: Schirmer Trade Books, 2005.

Krasilovsky, M. William, Sydney Shemel, and John M. Gross. *This Business of Music: The Definitive Guide to the Music Industry*. 9th ed. New York: Billboard Books, 2003.

Kusek, Dave, and Gerd Leonhard. *The Future of Music: Manifesto for the Digital Music Revolution*. Boston: Berklee Music Press, 2005.

Lathrop, Tad. *This Business of Music Marketing and Promotion: A Practical Guide to Creating a Completely Integrated Marketing and E-Marketing Campaign*. Rev. ed. New York: Billboard Books, 2003.

Lydon, Michael. *Songwriting Success: How to Write Songs for Fun and (Maybe) Profit*. New York: Routledge, 2004.

Marcone, Steven. *Managing Your Band: Artist Management, the Ultimate Responsibility*, 4th ed. Wayne, NJ: High Marks, 2006.

Mitchell, Billy. *The Gigging Musician: How to Get, Play, and Keep the Gig*. San Francisco: Backbeat Books, 2001.

Moore, Steve. *The Truth about the Music Business: A Grassroots Business and Legal Guide*. Boston: Thomson Course Technology, 2005.

Pattison, Pat. *Writing Better Lyrics*. Boston: Berklee Music Press, 1995.

Poe, Randy. *The New Songwriter's Guide to Music Publishing*. 3rd ed. Cincinnati: Writer's Digest Books, 2005.

Rapaport, Diane Sward. *How to Make and Sell Your Own Record*. 5th ed. New York: Prentice Hall, 1999.

Schulenberg, Richard. *Legal Aspects of the Music Industry: An Insider's View of the Legal and Practical Aspects of the Music Industry*. New York: Billboard Books, 2005.

Schwartz, Daylle Deanna. *I Don't Need a Record Deal! Your Survival Guide for the Indie Music Revolution*. New York: Billboard Books, 2005.

Shagen, Rena. *Booking and Tour Management for the Performing Arts*. New York: Allworth Press, 1996.

Shih, Patricia. *Gigging: A Practical Guide.* New York: Allworth Press, 2003.

Songwriter's Market. Cincinnati: Writer's Digest, 1979–.

Souvignier, Todd, and Gary Hustwit. *The Musician's Guide to the Internet.* 2nd ed. Milwaukee: Hal Leonard, 2002.

Staines, Bill. *The Tour: A Life between the Lines.* Philadelphia: Xlibris Corporation, 2003.

Taylor, Livingston. *Stage Performance.* New York: Pocket Books, 2000.

Webb, Jimmy. *Tunesmith: Inside the Art of Songwriting.* New York: Hyperion Press, 1998.

Weiss, Mitch, and Perri Gaffney. *Managing Artists in Pop Music.* New York: Allworth Press, 2003.

Weissman, Dick. *Songwriting: The Words, the Music, the Money.* Milwaukee: Hal Leonard, 2001.

Weissman, Dick. *The Music Business: Career Opportunities and Self-Defense.* 3rd rev. ed. New York: Three Rivers Press, 2003.

Weissman, Dick. *Making a Living in Your Local Music Market: Realizing Your Market Potential.* 3rd ed. Milwaukee: Hal Leonard, 2006.

Whitsett, Tim. *Music Publishing: The Real Road to Music Business Success.* 5th ed. Vallejo, CA: Mix Books, 2005.

Wimble, David. *The Indie Bible.* 6th ed. New York: Music Sales, 2004.

Wixen, Randall, D. *The Plain and Simple Guide to Music Publishing.* Milwaukee: Hal Leonard, 2005.

PERFORMING RIGHTS ORGANIZATIONS' WEB SITES

Note: All of the performing rights organizations have offices in various cities. Rather than print each address, below are their Web sites.

ASCAP: www.ascap.com

BMI: www.bmi.com

SESAC: www.sesac.com

Songwriters Guild of America (SGA): www.songwritersresources.network.com

The Music Connection: www.musicconection.com

American Federation of Musicians: www.afm.org. They have several hundred local offices in the United States and Canada.

NARAS (National Academy of Recording Arts and Sciences): www.grammy.com. NARAS has twelve branch offices.

Below are some Web sites for prospective film composers or songwriters who want to place songs on film or television. The first three listed are free, the others charge subscription fees.

www.inhollywood.com

www.mandy.com

www.LukeHits.com

www.filmmusic.net

www.productionweekly.com

www.taxi.com

Hollywood Music Directory: www.hcdonline.com. HMD periodically publishes listings of music supervisors as well as agents,
managers, and record company personnel.

Women in Music National Network: www.womeninmusic.com

New Music Weekly: www.newmusicweekly.com. NMW covers the
radio and music industry within its weekly magazine, Web site,
NMW mail and fax services. NMW was built by radio stations
who "break" the hits first. Telephone: 310-325-9997.

RADIO STATIONS THAT WILL PLAY YOUR MATERIAL

XM Radio—XMU/The R.A.D.A.R. Report: airing Thursday 9 P.M.
Eastern time.

http://www.radiounsigned.com

XM Radio Channel 15 "The Village," Mary Sue Touhey

1500 Eckington Plaza NE

Washington, D.C. 20002

Craig's Music: the radio voice of independent music

http://www.craigsmusic.net

Lime Light Radio: an independent online radio station that focuses
specifically on unsigned bands and solo artists.

http://www.limelightradio.com

Unsigned Underground

230 S. Main Street

Newtown, CT 06470

Telephone: 203-426-2030

FAX: 203-426-2036

Darryl Gregory info@unsignedunderground.net

www.unsignedunderground.net

This show is broadcast on WVOF 88.5 Fairfield University, Weds.
4 P.M. to 6 P.M. EST.

WRHO FM
Hartwick College
1 Hartwick Drive
Oneonta, NY 13820
Telephone: 607-431-4555
FAX: 607-431-4064
Alex Cameron wrho@hartwick.edu
http://users.hartwick.edu/wrho
"Please send us your promo CDs. We play all genres of music; however, we tend to lack the folk/country/jazz/blues/classical/ spoken word genres."

WGRX FM
4414 Lafayette Blvd. Ste #100
Fredericksburg, VA 22408
Telephone: 540-891-9696
FAX: 540-891-1656
Stephanie Taylor staylor@thunder1045.com
http://www.thunder1045.com
They program an Americana/bluegrass program.

This following listing of stations that will play your music is a good place for you to start assembling your own radio database. They all have independent programs in various genres, and they all broadcast *River City Folk* and other syndicated programming. Many of these Alaska stations listed below are particularly open to receiving artists' CDs. Many of the large independents and major labels do not service them, so they are more apt to give your CD a listen.

KBRW-FM
1695 Okpik Street
Box 109
Barrow, AK 99723
907-852-6811

KDLG-AM
670 Seward Street
Dillingham, AK 99576
907-842-5281

KHNS-FM
P. O. Box 1109
Haines, AK 99827
907-766-2020

KOTZ-AM
Kotzebue Broadcasting Inc.
Box 78
Kotxebue, AK 99752
907-442-3434

KSKO-AM
Mile 389, Iditarod Trail
P. O. Box 70
McGrath, AK 99627
907-524-3001

KSDP-AM
P. O. Box 328
Sand Point, AK 99661
907-383-5737

KTNA-FM
Box 300
Talkeetna, AK 99676
907-733-1700

KIAL-AM
P. O. Box 181
Unalaska, AK 99685
907-581-1888

KCHU-AM
128 Pioneer Drive
P. O. Box 467
Valdez, AK 99686
907-835-4665

KSTK-FM
202 St. Michael Street
P. O. Box 1141
Wrangell, AK 99929
907-874-2345

KXGA-FM (Glenallen)
Terminal Radio Inc.
P. O. Box 467
Valdez, AK 99686

KXKM-FM (McCarthy)
Terminal Radio Inc.
P. O. Box 467
Valdez, AK 99686

KXRJ
Arkansas Tech Universtiy
Wilson Hall, Hwy 7 North
Russellville, AR 72801

KUAR-FM
2801 South University Avenue
Little Rock, AR 72204
501-569-8485
Translators in:
    Monticello, AR
    Forest City, AR
    Hope, AR
    Batesville, AR

KAWC-FM
9500 S. Avenue 8E
Yuma, AZ 85366
602-344-7690

WKGC-FM
5230 West Highway 98
Panama City, FL 32401
904-769-5241

WXEL-FM
P. O. Box 6607
West Palm Beach, FL 33404
407-737-8000

WPRK
Rollins College
Dan Seeger
1000 Holt Avenue
Winter Park, FL 32789

WUGA-FM
The Georgia Center for Continuing Education
University of Georgia
Athens, GA 30602
706-542-9842

KTPR-FM
330 Avenue M
Fort Dodge, IA 50501
515-955-5877

KBSU-FM
1910 University Drive
Boise, ID 83725
208-385-3663

WDCB-FM
Lambert Road and 22nd Street
Glen Ellyn, IL 60137
630-942-4200
This is an excellent station to send CDs to; they have a wide variety of programs, and generally listen to every CD they receive.

WEIV-FM
Eastern Illinois University
600 Lincoln Avenue
1521 Buzzard Hall
Charleston, IL 61920
Rick Sailors

WEPS-FM
Ken Huske
355 East Chicago St.
Elgin, IL 60120

WKYU-FM
Academic Complex
1 Big Red Way
Western Kentucky University
Bowling Green, KY 42101
502-745-5489
Repeating stations in:
    WKUE-FM Elizabethtown
    WKPB-FM Henderson
    WDCL-FM Somerset

WNKU-FM
301 Landrum
Northern Kentucky University
Highland Heights, KY 41099
606-572-6500

KSLU-FM
Tennessee and Sycamore Streets
SLU Box 783
University Station
Hammond, LA 70402
504-549-2330

WFWM-FM
Rene Atkinson
Frostburg State University
Stangle Bldg
Frostburg, MD 21532

WUMB-FM
University of Massachusetts, Harbor Campus
100 Morrissey Boulevard
Boston, MA 02125
617-287-6900
(Twenty-four hours a day of independent-label and artist-label music)
Repeaters in:
    WBPR, Worcester, MA
    WFPB, Falmouth, MA

WOMR 92.1 FM
Cape Cod
P. O. Box 975
Provincetown, MA 02657
508-921-WOMR

KRCU-FM
One University Plaza
Cape Girardeau, MO 63701
314-651-5070

KUMR-FM
G-6 Library
University of Missouri
Rolla, MO 65401
314-341-4386

KEMC-FM
1500 North 30th St.
Billings, MT 59101
406-657-2941
Repeaters in:
    KBMC-FM, Bozeman, MT
    KNMC-FM, Havre, MT
    KECC-FM, Miles City, MT
Translators in:
    Big Sky, MT
    Big Timber, MT
    Buffalo, WY
    Chester/Sweet Grass MT
    Cody, WY
    Columbus, MT
    Cutbank, MT
    Forsythe, MT
    Glasgow, MT
    Glendive, MT
    Greybull, WY
    Hardin, MT
    Helena, MT
    Lewiston, MT
    Livingston, MT
    Lovell, WY
    Powell, WY
    Red Lodge, MT
    Shelby, MT
    Sheridan, WY
    Thermopolis, WY
    Two River, MT
    Worland, WY
    Yellowstone, WY

KIOS-FM
Omaha, NE

KUCV-FM
1800 North 33rd Street
Lincoln, NE 68503
402-472-3611
Repeaters in:
    KCNE-FM, Chadron, NE

KHNE-FM, Hastings, NE
KLNE-FM, Lexington, NE
KMNE-FM, Bassett, NE
KPNE-FM, North Platte, NE
KRNE-FM, Merriman, NE
KTNE-FM, Alliance, NE
KXNE, Norfolk, NE
KZUM Community Radio, Lincoln, NE

KSJE-FM
4601 College Boulevard
Farmington, NM 87402
505-599-0517

WSKG-FM
P. O. Box 3000
Binghamton, NY 13902
607-729-0100
Repeaters in:
    WSQC-FM, Oneonta, NY
    WSQE-FM, Corning, NY
    WSQG-FM, Ithaca, NY

WHPC-FM
Nassau Community College
One Education Drive
Garden City, NY 11530
516-572-7439

WGWG-FM
Jeff Powell
106 Emily Lane
Boiling Springs, NC 28017

WLHS
6840 Lakota Lane
Liberty Township, OH 45044
513-759-4163

WCHE-FM
105 W. Gay Street
Westchester, PA 19380
Ron Johnson

WMCE
Mercyhurst College/Baldwin Hall
501 East 38th Street
Erie, PA 16546

KESD-FM
Telecommunications Center
P. O. Box 5000
Vermillion, SD 57069
605-677-5861
Repeaters in:
    KCSD-FM, Sioux Falls, SD
    KDSD-FM, Pierpont, SD
    KESD-FM, Brookings, SD
    KPSD-FM, Faith, SD
    KQSD-FM, Lowry, SD
    KTSD-FM, Reliance, SD
    KZSD-FM, Martin, SD

WAPX-FM
Austin Peay State University
681 Summer Street, Shafteen Bldg.
Clarksville, TN 37040

WEVL-FM
Brian Craig
518 South Main Street
Memphis, TN 38103

WKTS-FM
Nancy Beth Gerberding
410 N. Kentucky Street
Kingston, TN 37763

KACU, Abilene, Texas

KSHU-Sam Houston Universtiy
Communications Bldg.
RM 123
Huntsville, TX 77340
Russell Fielder

KUSU-FM
Utah Public Radio
Utah State University
Logan, UT 84322
801-797-3138

Translators in:
  Bear Lake
  Brigham City
  Cedar City
  Delta
  Duchesne
  Grace, Idaho
  Hanksville
  Milford
  Nephi
  Panguitch
  Parowan
  Provo
  Randolf-Woodward
  Richfield
  Soda Springs
  St. George
  Tabiona
  Teasdale
  Vernal
  Zion National Park

WHRV-FM
5200 Hampton Boulevard
Norfolk, VA 23508
804-889-9400

WVRU
Ashley Claud
P. O. Box 6973
Radford, VA 24142

WBSD
Tom Tyler
400 McCanna Parkway
Burlington, WI 53105

OTHER MEDIA RESOURCES

M3 Radio
Attn: Tony-O/Music Dir.
259 West 30th Street
12th Floor
New York City, NY 10001
www.M3Radio.com

The Indie Bible: a compilation of resources for independent song-writers. http://www.indiebible.com/usasong

The Music Business registry: accurate, up-to-the minute contact information for A&R, music publishers, record producers, music attorneys, and music supervisors. http://www.musicregistry.com

NACA: perform live for thousands of student buyers and their advisors from colleges across the country. http://www.naca.org

MusicGorilla.com: label and publisher placement. http://www.MusicGorilla.com

Overplay: music site dedicated to the development and exposure of emerging artists/bands. Overplay give artists the platform to be seen and heard and the tools to sell their music online. http://www.overplay.com

Doak Turner's Nashville newsletter: sent to over 10,000 songwriters and music industry professionals every week. Good songwriter's resource. http://www.nashvillemuse.com

Australian Country Music Listeners Association: http://www.acmla.com.au

New Music Weekly: http://www.newmusicweekly.com

Loggins Radio Promotion: http://www.logginspromotion.com

Mediaguide: proprietary technology monitors nearly 2,500 U.S. radio stations twenty-four hours a day, seven days a week. http://www.artistmonitor.com

Hal Leonard: http://www.halleonard.com

Ibanez: http://www.ibanez.com

Sony: http://www.sonystyle.com

Livewire Contacts: http://www.livewiremusician.com

IK Multimedia: http://www.ikmultimedia.com

Onlinegigs: the only fully automated booking and promotional tool for today's music industry. http://www.onlinegigs.com

Songsalive: a nonprofit organization supporting and promoting songwriters and composers worldwide. http://www.songsalive.org

MAGAZINES

Singout!
www.singout.org

> *Singout!* is a quarterly magazine that offers a songwriting advice column and much more about the art of songwriting. *Singout!* also lists a complete rundown of music festivals in the United States, featuring all types of roots music.

Performing Songwriter
www.performingsongwriter.com

> *Performing Songwriter* magazine covers all styles and genres of pop music. Songwriters such as Michael Johnson regularly contribute.

Dirty Linen
www.dirtylinen.com

> A magazine specializing in folk and all types of world music, in the United States and the United Kingdom.

Folk Roots
www.frootsmag.com

Roots, folk, and world music magazine, published in the United Kingdom. Includes articles, features, reviews, radio.

FESTIVALS

In addition to these festivals, there are literally hundreds, if not thousands, more throughout the United States, Canada, and overseas. These festivals are good places to start, but consult the resources above, newspapers, and other periodicals in your area for opportunities near you.

Northwest Festival Guide
www.northwestfestivalguide.com
Festival listings for Oregon, Washington, Idaho, and Montana.

Kerrville Folk Festival
www.kerrville-music.com

> The largest singer/songwriter/performer gathering in the United States. It takes place beginning Memorial Day weekend every year and continues for the eighteen days following that holiday. Though there are a few motels in Kerrville, nine miles away, virtually everyone camps at the Happy Valley Ranch, where the concerts take place and the songwriter campfires burn every evening.

Ontario Council of Folk Festivals
www.ocff.ca

> This is an umbrella organization for a number of diverse festivals in Ontario, Canada. The work "folk" is a very inclusive one there, including blues, world, and jazz music.

Rocky Mountain Folks Festival
Lyons, Colorado
www.efolkmusic.org

> This Colorado gathering is worth a special mention because of its excellent song school, and it also has a songwriting competition.

Sisters Folk Festival, Sisters, Oregon
www.sistersfolkfestival.com

This festival takes place the weekend after Labor Day each September, and is an intimate affair in a charming western town. It also offers a comprehensive song school where the attendees live in teepees for a few days. The winner of the songwriting competition receives a quality Breedlove guitar, among other prizes.

Vancouver Folk Music Festival
www.thefestival.bc.ca/

> Largest folk and world music festival in western Canada. Jericho Beach Vancouver, British Columbia, in mid-July.

Walnut Valley Festival
Winfield, Kansas
www.wvfest.com/

> This is probably the largest gathering of musicians and songwriters in mid-America each year, in late September.

ABOUT THE AUTHORS

TOM MAY

In his 34 years as a professional singer/songwriter/performer, Tom May has touched hundreds of thousands of lives with his songs through his concerts across the United States and overseas; with his weekly radio program, *River City Folk,* heard on more than 200 stations and XM satellite radio; and his work on events that benefit entire communities and states, such as Winterfolk (Portland, Oregon's largest annual folk music event, which May founded and directs).

He has recorded eleven albums for various labels, featuring selections from his own song catalog, which number well over 200 songs. He has also produced albums for other artists; directed numerous festivals in the northwest United States and elsewhere; and served on the national board of directors for the Folk Alliance, an organization based in Washington, D.C., to promote traditional music and dance.

May has performed in every state in the union, as well as in Canada, England, Ireland, Scotland, Germany, and Belgium. His performing venues have included prestigious concert halls, small-town auditoriums, and humble coffeehouses. His festival appearances include the Kerrville Folk Festival (Texas), the Napa Valley Folk Festival (California), Sisters Folk Festival (Oregon), the Juan De Fuca Festival (Port Angeles, Washington), and dozens more.

May's music was chosen to represent Nebraska at the National Arts Council's annual conference in 1994 and 1995 in South Carolina and Omaha. In September 1994, May headlined a special series of concerts with the Omaha Symphony Orchestra, one of the most acclaimed regional orchestras in the United States. He performed a set of his music with full orchestral accompaniment to capacity crowds and rave reviews. In 1997 and 1998, May did a series of concerts throughout Alaska in honor of the Klondike Gold Rush centennial.

Most recently, May traveled back to his hometown of Omaha, Nebraska, to perform a very special show for the 125th anniversary of Creighton University, featuring a song he composed for the occasion.

May has toured with and opened for many well-known artists, including Gordon Lightfoot, Alabama, Willie Nelson, and many others. He currently performs and tours solo or with his acoustic trio.

In addition to his live concert appearances, May has appeared on dozens of radio and television programs: National Public Radio's syndicated *Mountain Stage;* Radio Eirhenn's (Ireland) Andy O'Mahoney show, and the CBC's *Ian Tyson Show* (television) to name a few.

May also produces and hosts his own national radio/TV broadcast, *River City Folk.* The show is heard weekly on more than 200 radio stations and on XM Satellite Radio from Alaska to New York. *River City Folk* highlights the vitality of the acoustic music scene by featuring diverse performers and styles. The radio version of *River City Folk* remains one of the premier showcases for acoustic singer/songwriters nationally, and celebrated its twenty-first anniversary in 2006.

You can find out more about Tom May's touring, radio program, and other projects at www.tommayfolk.com, or contact him at rcftommay@msn.com.

DICK WEISSMAN

Dick Weissman is a musician, composer, and author who has worked in a variety of capacities in the music industry. He has done hundreds of recording sessions and performances, and was a founding member of the legendary folk-pop group, the Journeymen, along with Scott McKenzie and John Phillips. Weissman has written more than 100 recorded songs and instrumental pieces, as well as two feature film scores, and songs and instrumental music for three plays.

He is the author of fourteen published books about music and the music business, including the best-selling *The Music Business: Career*

Opportunities and Self-Defense. For further information, you can go to his Web site at www.dickweissman.com.

CHRIS KENNEDY

Chris Kennedy is an occasional folksinger, guitarist, and speaker when he is not in the classroom as an associate professor of communication at Western Wyoming Community College in Rock Springs.

INDEX